Dedication

This book is dedicated to production supervisors in the food processing industry. Many of the stories in this book contain accounts that describe their demanding job. In my experience of over 20 years in Food Processing, I can say that we all owe those most key people in food processing a debt of gratitude for caring about their work. Because of them, we can go to the grocery store, and expect to buy commercially safe food products. Thank you. Be proud of what you do.

Foreword

I spent over 20 years working for four different food processing companies, making thousands of different products. I have a lot of stories. The stories are not in any chronological order.

I wrote this because I did not want to become one of those old guys who repeat the same stories over and over to people who heard them already and are too polite to walk away. So I figured I should write these tasty tales of bungling for posterity. That way, they can just go get a copy of this book and I can spare them the oral version.

Disclaimer

Don't blame any of today's workers on what was done in any of the stories mentioned here. I have not been in the Food Processing Industry for 15 years. The companies have changed hands and the same people are not there. I changed all the names.

Rancid Tales

My years in the Food Processing Industry

© 2014 by Den Warren

Also by Den Warren: *KINGS and CLANS of the Midwest*

A dystopian novel depicting the US dollar collapse, causing an apocalyptic breakdown of the economy. The result is people fighting over limited resources.

Factions are populated by colorful characters who engage in conflict for their survival. Unlike many novels in this genre, tension builds as everyone does not get along all of the time, and everything does not go right all the time.

The novel is fast-moving, action-packed and entertaining. This is book one of a planned series. Thank you for considering it.

Den Warren

Operation Misfortune Cookie

One of the many jobs I did while in the food industry was working as a Tech in a quality lab. My primary function in that particular lab was to assure the quality of our products.

One of our many products at that Company was fortune cookies. The cookies were produced for us by another company as a pass-through item. The niche item was processed by a small Chinese-American bakery, but we would still validate the quality of the cookies as they bore our brand logo.

Don was a guy who always came into the lab to "check" the quality report of the particular line he was on, but not really in charge of. This follow-up by him should have really only taken a few seconds a day. Unless he was really mad at me, which sometimes happened, he would come into the air conditioned lab to take refuge from the heat for ten to twenty minutes.

Don was always snacking, and he would munch on the test cookies when a sample box was being inspected. These got thrown out anyway.

Then Don would check his fortune. These fortunes were always very fortuitous. In fact, I had heard that we had a lawyer look them over before they were published in the cookie to make sure the Company could not be liable for whatever it said.

Rancid Tales

Don was the ignorant sort who believed in the authenticity of the spontaneity of professional wrestling. Don spent his entire lifetime not really wanting to learn anything productive.

Don's brother-in-law worked in the same place, on the same shift. When it came to Don, his brother-in-law was a one man truth squad. The brother-in-law would tell us that Don was lying about his military service; about being from Kentucky; on and on. But then, I couldn't say if his brother-in-law was totally trustworthy either. Don's brother-in-law was a hair trigger hothead, beyond anything someone would want to taunt or confront.

Don was also given to much drama. At least once, maybe twice, he demolished his television after a Dallas Cowboys loss. I used to tell him before a game that he needed to put chicken wire in front of his TV.

Don's dramatic unpredictability tended to intimidate the newer workers, and he knew it, so he would play the bully. But as factory life is so boring, a dramatic person can be of some real entertainment value, and make the time pass more bearably. So naturally, some of us would proactively seek to prompt a dramatic display from him. Once the newer guys saw us clowning on him, they would relax.

The best way to taunt Don was to disparage one of his sports teams. He never went for the local teams, which in a rural area means within a three hour drive. Don only went for teams with a solid sustained winning history. I guess that somehow that made him a winner personally.

Den Warren

All anyone had to do was to badmouth his wrestling show or NASCAR to get his goat. We even badmouthed things he liked whether we liked them or not. We took any kind of a stand that we couldn't care less about just to make him mad.

Another easy way to goad him was by ripping on Democrats. He had no concept why he was aligned with Democrats, in fact he talked like a conservative, but he hated Republicans. He knew who he hated. No matter what you asked him, you couldn't get a straight intelligent answer from him.

This time in the lab I was ready for him. I took some forceps and slipped out the "nothing is ever wrong in the unicorn, butterfly, bluebird, rainbow world" paper fortune from among its unyielding crispy fold. I surgically inserted another fortune of my own composition, that was printed in the same fortune cookie red ink.

"The Lakers will lose tonight."

The Lakers were involved in a best-of-seven series with another team, whom I forget. The Lakers were heavy favorites. Of course, the Lakers were one of Don's teams.

I placed the Laker cookie on the edge of the tray, a little off by itself. It was in the perfect position for someone of low energy to nab.

As expected, Don came into the lab. He did not seem interested in the cookies for some reason. All that effort for nothing.

He was in a loitering mood though, and after leaning on the table near the tray, he eventually decided upon a little snack. Bingo. He grabbed the right cookie.

I figured he would get a little sore at being punked, which was of course, the objective. Then he would give me the business, and I could laugh at his drama and tell everyone about the ploy.

He opened the cookie and read the fortune. His eyes got as big as half-dollars. He started choking on the crispy treat. I was waiting for him to start yelling at me.

Instead, he was actually taking the fortune to heart. Given his tendencies, I shouldn't have expected anything different.

"Is something wrong, Don?"

He read the fortune again to himself in astonishment. "Hmmm...That must be the first sports fortune I have seen."

This was way better than expected. He was seriously worried over the cookie, and the night's game.

Since the ruse was not over, I had to go along with it until its conclusion, as did everyone else who knew about it.

Don's arch-nemesis, Willie, was telling him that he also went into the lab and got a fortune cookie. Willie said the cookie read that another one of Don's teams was going to lose. Willie said Don was really squirming, and did not respond.

I feared Willie's greedy overplaying the ploy would ruin the whole thing, but it seemed there was no limit to Don's gullibility.

Den Warren

As it turned out, strangely enough, the Lakers *did* lose that game. In fact, they lost four in a row and lost the series they were supposed to win. It almost caused us to take pause. . . okay, not really.

Don feared the innocent looking cookies with their sinister reality altering fortunes within, and passed on eating them for quite awhile after that. But even his refusals were in a dramatic fearful fashion, which also provided bonus fun. So I kept up the warnings of caution.

Surreal: During my years I was exposed to quite a bit of food science. But it seemed wrong to me when very good cooks would ask me questions about food, such as shelf life or heat penetration. I have been able to answer their questions. It's just good that they don't ask me to inspect their kitchen. I'm certain they wouldn't like it. I have taken up cooking myself and am passable at it.

Mysterious Slamming

I was working in a small room that made the "skins" to egg rolls. It was a new operation at the time. I handled the actual skin making machine. Another operator ran the dough mixer.

Every once in awhile we would hear this slamming noise. It was loud enough to startle us. We looked around and everything would be totally normal. Maybe a couple of hours later it would do it again.

The mysterious slamming would occur every day. In fact, it seemed to increase in frequency. This was getting to be a real distraction. The banging seemed to be coming from the direction of our stainless steel starch holding tank mounted on the wall. The tank had about a 40 gallon capacity.

We did not have the slightest clue what to do about the annoyance. We reported this condition, but when the anomaly did not affect the process and was only a pain to us, it went on largely ignored.

It didn't help that my co-worker in the room was maybe the biggest complainer who I have ever met. No one wanted to work with her. In fact, I'm pretty sure that because it was her, that they were all glad we were having the problem. Personally, I had no problem working with her.

Den Warren

Being in the Skin room was otherwise a pretty good job, I thought. I would stay on a job until I got bored with it, then I would just change jobs within the Company.

One day when the bang occurred, the Dough Mixer Operator yelled out. I remember not being able to get out of her what was going on. She said something about a spark. After that, she had no inclination to go near my machine. Her mind-set did not give me a warm and fuzzy feeling about my proximity to the starch bin. I kept watching her to see where she was looking.

One day this thing was popping like crazy so I kept watching for it. "Whoa!" There was a three foot long streak of blue lightning that jumped from the outside of a PVC pipe that pulled recycled starch from the line into the tank.

We studied the crazy phenomenon. The zapping was static electricity generated from starch sucking through the pipe. The micro-lightning jumping to the tank caused a dust explosion inside the tank. The slamming was the heavy stainless steel lid of the starch tank popping up with the explosion and slamming down with gravity.

Maybe the increase in explosions that day was due to a lack of humidity in the skin room or something. Conditions were just right for it though. I turned off the light in the room so people passing by could see the fantasia that was our work area. It was indeed a glorious display. It attracted quite a bit of attention as people were standing around being unproductive on the clock beholding its awesomeness.

Finally, the drain on human resources warranted some attention by supervision. Maintenance sent a guy over to figure out what to do. He was baffled and did not believe us until he saw it. He ended up running a grounding wire from the pipe to the floor. This solved the problem. He explained that the static electricity did not have much voltage, but had like, a million amps. We did not miss having it around.

Parking Lot Intervention

I was in the parking lot walking into work. I heard a scream and some slamming. I ran over and saw a guy who was a crew leader. He was slamming a woman up against the now caved-in fender of a pickup truck.

I pulled the guy off of her, and told him to stop. He gave me a shove, after which I just looked at him. He backed off after that.

The owner of the truck was really mad about his truck.

That was pretty much it. I was called into the office and gave my report. The woman beater got fired. The woman went to the hospital, and when she got out, she said I saved her life. We'll never know if that was true or not.

Den Warren

Literally Pushing His Button

I was in filling in for the second shift production manager. I was in the production office doing the production paperwork when the phone rang. It was a guy who came to the company to deliver a bulk tanker of soy sauce. He said that I needed to call Ned from Receiving to unload it.

I told the driver that Ned was on day shift and had just left. He said that Ned always unloads it. I went back to see if I could avoid bothering Ned by doing something myself about it. I asked him what was involved with unloading it. He said that he hooked the hose up and all that I had to do was check the connection and push the button to the pump.

So I checked the connection and pushed the button. The deliveryman gave me a strange look.

"That's it?" I asked, since the driver made me wonder.

"That's it."

Okay. That's overly simple, I thought, so I went back to the paperwork.

A little while later Ned broke my concentration by screaming and cussing at me at the top of his lungs. "Why are you doing my job?"

"What? Because I pushed one button?"

He was still throwing a world class tantrum. Obviously to try and intimidate and bully me. He was the Chief Union Steward and no doubt felt that it was his place to be the tough guy.

I realized that this deliveryman knew about the smelly arrangement. Ned could have "unloaded" the soy sauce on his regular shift. He just wanted call back pay to come back and do nothing.

I stood my ground. I told him, "We are not going to call you in and give you four hours of pay just to push one button." He obviously knew the tanker was coming in so he could have stayed over and done some real work for an hour until the tanker arrived.

Ned stormed out of the office with determination. He headed down the hall. No doubt he went to cry to one of the big dogs about how he was going to file a grievance. I thought that maybe my stand would only confirm to upper management that I would not yield to such tactics and they would see that as a plus.

I readied myself for a battle that I had no intention whatsoever of losing. Strangely enough, I never heard one word of this again. Ned may have had a deal with management on this. In which case, I should have ratted his arrangement to his rank and file members. Maybe he realized his stance would not be acceptable and he would not prevail. On top of that, I would write him up for his screaming and cussing at me.

One of the few regrets I have from those days is that I did not more aggressively pursue writing him up. I was a Union Steward once. I knew that pasting Ned with a write-up that stuck would be a big torpedo to the hull of his big battleship sized ego. On the other hand, I did not feel that I had firm backing from a wavering management.

Years later after this occurrence, I related this story to another guy at a different company. He threw a big fit saying that I took this guy's job. Perhaps you as the reader agree that I was in the wrong. "Nuts" to you.

I maintain that this evil practice of featherbedding is nothing short of legalized extortion and jeopardized the health and longevity of the company.

Lock Out Tag Out: The sanitation supervisor wanted to find who had the lock on the panel that was for the big mixer across the room so she could start it. The owner of the lock was nowhere to be found so she went and got the big bolt cutters and cut the lock. Then the guy who was cleaning the mixer hopped out of it a couple of seconds before she got it started. We were still worried there might be a fatality.

Crybaby Don

Author's Note: This is the same Don mentioned in the story "Misfortune Cookie".

Don was a very ambition-challenged worker. He had a job that could be done while leaning most of the time. The real lazy part comes in where he finally after all of that leaning, should have been doing something, but still maintained a static state of inactivity.

One of my numerous jobs at this food processing company was to prepare egg roll ingredients for frozen egg rolls. We would run hundreds of pounds of meat and vegetables through a slicer. Then we would weigh out the ingredients into stainless steel barrels. Then flip the barrels into a vat of boiling water. After that, we raked the vegetables into a conveyor.

We were busy all the time. We did hard physical work with all of the lifting. We were young and strong so it was a decent job for us. There was not so much in the way of headaches on the job.

Yet Don was a big pain. We would page him to bring mung bean sprouts to us which was about all of the physical activity Don would ever see. The sprouts would arrive in large wheeled tubs about the size of a compact car. It took some effort to move them.

Don knew that if he would ignore us long enough, to keep the line from going down, we would go all the way over there and get the tubs ourselves, then bring back the empties for him. Don was also supposed to pick the empties up. When we did bring them back, we would see Don leaning on some equipment, and looking at it as if it would not run and needed his expert attention.

Den Warren

This behavior caused us to become very disappointed in Don.

Sometimes we chose to leave his empty tubs pile up in our department. A couple of times we moved them to the far side of the department so he would have to go get them. That really tweaked him off.

On other occasions we would take the abundance of tubs back all at once.

Don would say, "Set it over there."

Instead we belligerently jammed them all right in his way so he couldn't move. He was red hot. We put water from the drinking fountain into our fists and them rubbed our eyes like we were crying, with water running down.

"WAH!"

Everyone in his department was hooting and laughing at him. People in Don's department, other than him, worked extremely hard. They worked even harder than us, and Don did nothing to help them out.

Whenever we would page Don at lunch time for full tubs, he would come back over the loudspeaker, "I'm at lunch!" The pages both ways could be heard all over the plant. My partner and I took a liking to hearing him yell on the intercom. So if we needed some sprouts near his lunch time, we would wait a bit after we called to see if he would yell. He never disappointed. Then when he did bring the tanks over, he would slam them into the wall or equipment to show his disapproval of us.

One time I boldly paged Don while he was at lunch and waited a few seconds.

He screamed the obligatory, "I'm at lunch!"

Then I came back with a page, "Next time check to see if we need any before you go." That got the supervisor's attention since he knew Don would be furious. So, the supervisor told me that was not an appropriate page. I asked him if it would be appropriate for him to yell at us over the intercom when he should have supplied us. The supervisor said he would straighten it out.

Boy was Don mad when he brought the sprouts over. He almost slammed them into the line. He would have been a cooked goose if that would have happened. We showed our empathy for his plight by pointing at him and laughing as hard as possible.

Kosherization: At one company we paid to have a rabbi come in and declare an item was kosher so we could get their seal. Sometimes the Company would choose to ignore their blessing and run without it. Not my call. Realistically though, our cleaning process was far superior to what they expected.

Den Warren

Canadian Adventure

My first regular job in the food processing industry as a sanitor. A sanitor is a person who cleans the production equipment to a spotless condition. It was not too bad of a job to have at the time. Almost the whole crew were either Mexicans, or Mexican-Americans. At least one guy was from Puerto Rico.

I got along real well with most of them. Some became close friends. We would play softball, touch football, and basketball. I even had a wrestling match with Armando, who was an accomplished State wrestler in high school. Though he was smaller, he surprised me with a quick takedown. It was all I could handle to keep up with him and I had to concede a loss to him.

I went to the Latin-American club, and we would go to each others' social events. Armando was to be in my wedding party in a few months.

Our shift would get over at about 10:30 pm. It was Friday night and we seldom had to work Saturday or stay late at that job. We were in the restroom and I was looking at my infected tonsils in the mirror. I kept getting tonsillitis and was finally getting over it. Armando was there with Dan, another Mexican-American.

They asked me if I wanted to go to Canada.

"Huh? When?"

"After work."

"Tonight? With no sleep? You guys are crazy."

"We've never been there and we thought maybe you would go with us to help us get around. But we're worried about being up there on the Fourth of July."

"The Fourth of July is the US birthday, goof ball. You are going to Canada."

"Oh. . .yea."

I thought, how crazy! But I had the misconception that soon I would be married and I would not be able to do impulsive crazy fun things any more.   The truth is that you won't *want* to do stupid stuff like that when you get older.

So I called up my beautiful bride-to-be and told her that I was going on this ill-conceived trip to Canada. She didn't mind at all.

After work we got our stuff and camping gear and piled it into Armando's Volkswagen Beetle and hit the road. It was only a few hours on the road for us to cross the bridge into Canada. By then it was clear to me that Armando and Dan knew nothing about navigating with a road map, among other travel related things.

We got to the border. The Canadian Customs Agent greeted us. Back then they were all friendly old guys at the border. Those guys were pretty cool. Years later it seemed like Canada was guarded by a bunch of cranky women.

"Where 'ya goin'? the Customs Agent asked.

Armando spoke up, "Canada."

"Big Country," the Agent said without the least indication that he was annoyed by the inadequate response.

Den Warren

We had no clue where in Canada we were going. Armando and Dan sat there and looked at each other.

"Toronto," I blurted out from the cramped back seat. I had to sit back there since I was the tall one and couldn't fit well in the front of the bug.

The Border Agent was happy he got some kind of an answer out of us and let us go without much bother. We told him where we were born, etc.

Soon we celebrated the fact we were in Canada. We were still wide awake, having had no sleep.

We were past due for breakfast. We stopped at a restaurant in Rodney, Ontario and had a good breakfast. We wondered why all of the tables in the restaurant had vinegar on them. We learned that Canadians liked vinegar on their fish and chips, which to us was deep fried fish in a basket with French fries.

The next order of business was to find a campsite, as we were fading fast. I brought a travel book along that listed campsites. This was in the days long before smart phones.

"Hey! Look at that road!" Armando exclaimed.

The road we were on was heading right toward a mountain. This was not just a hill, but a mountain, and the road was not winding, but straight up. The grade was incredibly steep. I told Armando to get some momentum to go up the thing.

In retrospect, even that was a foolhardy suggestion. We were in a fully loaded VW Beetle. Going up for the first half was okay.

The little car started groaning under the weight. Armando downshifted the manual transmission.

At one point I thought we were going to start rolling backwards all the way back down. He downshifted again. The car heaved and jerked, but crept forward. There was still a ways to go.

Okay, I thought, we are going to die stupidly. We were going slow enough that Dan, who was on the front passenger side, thought about bailing out. But the bug crept along and eventually got to the top of the hill. What a relief!

We travelled to a couple of campgrounds and found that they were all booked up. I did not expect this situation. It seemed that camping was pretty popular.

Then we were pleased after I located a campground that had a sign outside of the office that said, "campsites available". Armando and Dan spared me the torment of climbing out of the back and went to the office. It was an agonizing wait. They were taking forever. I lost faith in them and climbed out to see what was going on.

The owner told me, "We are a family campground. We don't allow it."

"Allow what?" Whatever objectionable thing it was that he thought we were going to do, we certainly were too tired to do it.

He just kept saying, "We don't allow it."

I was about to ask him if he was a parrot. I was starting to get angry. I didn't know if he thought we were fugitives from the law, or because they were Mexicans, or gay, or druggies, or what the malfeasance was. We just weren't "family" enough. So I started to lecture him on sending us away all tired on the road and Armando and Dan pulled me away.

Maybe they were used to that sort of treatment, but I had never experienced it. I really felt like I had an idea of what it was like to be mistreated because of ethnic origin. I didn't like it one bit. True or not, I can see why people sometimes blame questionable actions on someone's bigotry.

The fatigue was really setting in after that. I could not stay awake.

I woke up and asked Armando why we were going so fast.

He said, "We can go a hundred."

So then I had to explain the difference between miles and kilometers. I pointed out that the kilometers/hr. was marked on the inner scale of his analog speedometer.

"Oh. I wondered what that was."

Dan was our navigator. He sucked. He got mad a couple of times when I showed him on the map we were going the wrong way, or at least a direction other than he thought.

At this point I was frequently falling asleep. I woke up and saw Armando was about asleep at the wheel. I tried to keep him awake for awhile then I fell asleep.

Another time I woke up and asked Dan where we were. He said with all assurance that we were on route such-and-such and knew exactly where we were. At the next moment we passed a road sign.

"Then how come the sign says. . ."

Dan yelled in frustration.

"Give me the road map," I said.

Eventually we found a place to camp. We could put our tent wherever we wanted. So we started setting up next to a recreational vehicle.

We were about finished setting up when a woman came out of the RV and said, "Why don't you guys move over there." She pointed down the hill.

"What for?" I asked her.

"I just think you should move down there."

This crap was really getting on my nerves. Again, Armando and Dan just told me we were going to move down there and forget it. I had that feeling again. If these people cannot tell you their reasons, their motivations must not be very good.

Armando could sleep anywhere. He laid flat out on his back on the grass and slept well. Dan and I did not do quite so well, but we got a little sleep.

Later that day the camp was completely filled up. I asked a guy if it was normal for the camp to be so full. He said that people celebrate the Fourth of July for the US, and the 1st, which is Canada's Day, the Canadian equivalent. But the first is a floating holiday, so it was a long weekend and the National Holiday of Canada. Yeesh! The knuckleheads were right after all! It was a bad weekend to be camping.

We saw that we needed some gas for the stingy bug. The owners of the camp were French Canadians. It was funny because the woman who sold us some gas from their pump was speaking to Dan in Canadian French, and Dan was speaking to her in Spanish, and they were understanding each other somewhat.

So far, we had not done anything except become totally exhausted. So I got the idea to go to Niagara Falls. Everyone likes to see the Falls. That would be the highlight we needed to make the it a real trip.

So we slept all day and woke up at night and took off for the Falls. We had to travel some distance to get there.

Not long after we were on the road, Armando mentioned excitedly, "Look at this big hill ahead!"

"Slow down!" I pleaded. "We can't see the bottom of the hill so we don't know how big it is!"

It was too late. It was that same mountain we struggled to go up before. Now we were going down. Armando was braking hard. I told him to let up, so the brakes didn't fail. By the time we got to the bottom we were flying super fast down the mountain like a toy Matchbox car down a plastic track.

After that harrowing experience, we made our way to Niagara Falls. It didn't disappoint. They were thrilled with the immensity of it. Nothing notably wrong happed there and it was a nice visit. No, really.

On the way back we pretty much did not want to look for a campsite any more. We crossed back into the US. Late at night, we found a New York State rest area listed on the map. When we got there it was big enough for about three cars total. We gave up and all three of us slept in the bug with our gear. It was a joke, but we were too tired to laugh.

A State Trooper found us there sleeping in the bug with our legs were sticking out of the windows. He told us that we were not supposed to be there since the park was closed. We told him we would leave, and he said for us to stay there until we woke up. That was a great kindness on his part.

We wanted to spend another day goofing off, so we found another campground in the US. It was a dirty place. The lake was muddy. We did not think much of it, but we stayed there.

We felt a void in our need to have fun, so on the way back we went to an Indiana State Park with a known nice beach. Armando was really dark. A lot of the darkness was a tan. Some black guys told him that he was darker than they were. The sun was no problem for them at all.

This was not the case for me. As a white guy, I was scorched to a crisp. Later that day after we got home, I was standing in the bathroom at the toilet and passed out. My sister heard the collapse and found me laying naked on the floor. My girlfriend was mad at me for not being able to go out that night as we had planned.

I was so sick that I missed work the next day and lost my holiday pay. Armando and Dan suffered no ill effects whatsoever. For a few years after that, whenever I was out for long in the sun, I felt sick. Eventually it went away.

Amphibian Horror

For a year or so, I was the crew leader of the celery inspection line. The celery was intensely washed and spread out on a wide conveyor belt for inspection. All I did was bring celery to the inspection line and take inspected celery to the production lines.

Our celery came from Florida. The fauna from Florida is quite different from our area.

Every once in awhile, I would hear a scream coming from the inspection area. The women were horrified because a frog or interesting lizard, or even a small fish would come down the line. Usually the small critters were alive and guys would take them home as pets.

The first time this happened the women ran away from the inspection belt. I got there before the little froggie was piped across the plant to the main production area. If this happened it could have easily ended up in the product.

I told the inspectors from that time forward, if they did not at least stop the belt the conveyor belt they would be sent home.

Even though they had plastic gloves on, they would never touch the animals. The downtime was usually for less than a minute so I put up with it. I didn't want any incentive for them to ignore the creatures.

Crappy Birthday to Me

I was on second shift as quality control. Second shift had the reputation for having a party-like atmosphere on our shift. Yet, I was busy all the time. So naturally, this perception about our shift and our work bothered me.

What is a party-like atmosphere? Webster's says a "party" by this meaning is a "gathering to which guests are invited in order to enjoy each other's company."

Okay, maybe in some sense it was. We would decide to eat dinner together. We would talk and laugh. Our lunch was a nice stress reducing respite. But we also got our work done, and things ran with good results.

One day, which happened to be my birthday, I was busy. I ran and ran and could not catch up enough to even have my lunch. This is probably why I have a touch of arthritis in my joints now.

My duties were not the sort of thing that could wait. My coworkers in the lab pleaded for me to stop and eat. They were nice enough to bring me a birthday cake. I ended up not getting any lunch but gulped a chunk of cake.

The next day, the Chief Operation Officer (COO) called me into his office. He started to lecture me on partying too much. Evidently someone was put out that the birthday party happened and they were not invited. Now that I think about it, it was probably Don.

I was irate and corrected his misconceptions for him. But after that no one wanted to have enjoyable lunches in the lab any more. We replaced having a small portion of time to unwind with contempt for our leadership. Just another lesson I learned on how not to handle situations.

Tricks and Traps

At one time I worked in a noodle production room. A guy I worked with was always running his mouth about things trying to agitate me for his own entertainment.

One day he and another guy took to setting traps for me. They were confounded by the fact I always knew they were up to something. For example; I disappointed them by anticipating that they had put a bag full of starch over the doorway. I opened the door, backed up, and the starch fell on the floor. I am not psychic. I could always tell by the goofy way they were acting that they were up to something.

So one day I decided to pay my arch-nemesis back. He sat all day in a small room. There was a square-foot opening by the floor. I got the help of his friend who tried to get me. He just wanted to play. I took a bag that was about the volume of a refrigerator. I put a couple of scoops of starch in it, because I knew he would cut the bag.

So I went around the put the bag into the opening on the floor. From the outside, I inflated it with an air hose. It got so big that he couldn't move in the room. Then as expected, he took his knife and stabbed the bag. The air pressure shot the corn starch out on him. He was all white with starch. It was real amusing, as well as satisfying. (Note: Horseplay often results in damage or injury.)

Rancid Tales

Top Ten Messes; Mess #10

Macaroni Guy

We made a popular line of frozen macaroni entrées. Most of them had pasta. I was a supervisor on second shift.

This evening, one of the lines I was supervising was processing one of our macaroni items. Cooked pasta was brought to us from the pasta line.

At the pasta line, an operator would take a stainless steel bucket and dip it into a bin of dry macaroni, then feed it into a stainless steel auger (like a big screw) filled with boiling water for about 11.5 minutes. About the same amount of time it takes you to boil it at home to get it done right.

The challenge of doing the job was more often than not trying to feed the pasta into the auger slow enough so the pasta did not stick together. Pasta that has stuck together is ruined, as it is undercooked from a lack of heat penetration where it stuck together. Also, clumped up pasta will not weigh right going down the line, and looks terrible. Of course on the other hand, if the operator fed the line too slowly, it would run the line out and cause downtime.

Another supervisor was in charge of the pasta area, which in turn supplied by entrée line. He was a fun guy to work with. He kind of reminded me of Squidward Tentacles. I know he would be offended by that, so I will just call him "Patrick".

Den Warren

We were always going through people at the Companies I supervised at. They worked too hard for the money they got. They worked way too many hours. Since the pay and conditions were so bad, we would always lose them to other industries that had better profit margins than the food industry. Consequently, the food processing industry was a very demanding place to supervise. You had to make a quality, commercially safe product, with generally a bottom of the pay scale work force. If you were not savvy enough to treat the good workers like gold, you would pay the price in short order.

One company I was with considered suspending the drug test requirement. Another one would bus workers in from the minimum security jail They tried all kinds of hiring bonuses and enticements.

Anyway, this was the pasta guy's first day on the job. Patrick was good at explaining a job very well. But he expected the young trainee to listen. Patrick made a point of telling the guy to pour very slowly and watched him do it for a bit.

Then after Patrick left, I saw the guy just cramming the pasta into the line with the bucket as fast as he could go. Huge globs of macaroni, about the size of a loaf of bread came flopping out on the auger into the stainless steel tub. I immediately got the guy to stop and contacted Patrick.

Patrick was irate at the ridiculous scene. He helped clear the waste by shoveling it into a scrap barrel and talked to the guy. "AGAIN. . .Do not feed the pasta in too fast. You can see what happens." Then Patrick had to leave because he was even more behind on his other chores.

A little time had passed. I glanced over at macaroni boy. Whoa! He's doing it again! The guy was flailing the bucket with a vengeance. I stopped the guy. Shaking my head, I got Patrick over there again.

"AGAIN... Do not feed the pasta too fast. You can see what happens." So the cleanup began again. Of course, we were accumulating downtime from the cleaning and refilling the pasta line.

Some time had passed. Lo and behold...yep...again. (You can't make this stuff up.) Patrick showed up and was jawing at the guy for some minutes while they scurried about. Then Patrick stood there and glared at his trainee with his arms folded for an extended period. He asked me to watch the nervous lad continuously while he made a call. Patrick called our manager at home, since we had destroyed a whole bin of macaroni. This amounted to a few hundred pounds of dry macaroni.

Patrick returned. "Well, I got the whole story. Evidently the new people we got today were from a special education institution and they are all mentally retarded. I told them it would be nice if they would have said something to us beforehand."

Sometimes we functioned more like a social institution than a business. Patrick and I both agreed that when we got a person like macaroni boy in to work, if we could somehow get them trained up on a task, they would be happy on a job others would find uninteresting, and they would stay there forever.

Happily, every day after that, the guy did do a pretty well. Once in awhile we would have to give him some feedback, but Macaroni Guy could be counted on to do a nice job.

Den Warren

Double Whammy

It was not too long after I started in the food industry. I had just missed a lot of work for being sick. Then a massive blizzard hits, which was actually two blizzards back to back. It was the worst snowstorm of my lifetime.

My car was parked in a lower level of a hill behind the house. By the time the snow was done, there was 6 feet of snow on top of the roof. The neighbor pulled my car out with his tractor.

Many people were stranded at work. You know it is bad if they can't make it home. For some reason, it is much harder to go to work than to go home.

After a day or so, Dad called from work, some 20 miles away and said he was going to try and make it home. We didn't have a snow blower, so I went out and shoveled the long drive. It was blowing shut about as fast as I could shovel.

Sure enough he accomplished the impressive feat and made it home. For years after that , I kept snow gear in my car so I could walk the five miles down the nearby railroad tracks home if I had to. To date, this had not happened.

The accounts of horseplay in this book were before I thought about someone getting hurt doing stunts like this. While amusing, horseplay is ill-advised. People do get seriously hurt from doing stupid stuff!

Rancid Tales

Top Ten Messes; Mess #9

Chicken Soup for the Landfill

It seems like there is always some cost to progress. There definitely was a downside to our new high speed line which would fill and seal soup cans at the rate of 400 cans per minute. This equals almost 7 cans per second. When you look at the line while it was running, it was almost a blur.

As the cans passed over the scale at this speed they were weighed with incredible accuracy. The scale had a display which was an average of 20 cans. Even this took some concentration to watch.

My job in quality control was to make sure that weight was being made on the cans of soup. The soup cans had to be filled with the correct amount of solids and liquid, but had to have an empty space at the top so when it went into the cooker, the bubble would stir the contents to insure commercial sterilization.

The line was very reliable. If a can did not make weight, a puff of compressed air would blow the can off of the conveyor into a barrel.

This was all fine, but often the filler would need adjusted. It takes some time to adjust the fill weights. You cannot just adjust it without it running at full speed.

Here is the problem; You are adjusting the line, and it only takes you a minute. You just sent 400 cans of soup flying off into a 55 gallon drum. It holds about 200.

It was not uncommon to go back to the line and see a thousand or so cans of soup in several barrels.

What if something was out of spec? If the condition lasted for 10 minutes, that was 4,000 cans. The line ran 192,000 cans a shift.

Looking at this situation, I recall the instant when I seriously questioned if I wanted that job any more.

The Game

I was a crew leader in a department at the time. We got unwelcome distractions of all kinds.

A woman who was helping our department from another department approached me while I was extremely busy. She said, "I don't like the game you're playing."

"What do you mean?"

"I don't like the game you're playing."

"What game? What are you talking about?"

"The GAME."

"Okay, I give up. I really don't know what you are talking about."

"You really don't, do you?

"No, I don't"

"Okay, never mind." Then she walked away.

Top Ten Messes; Mess #8

Chicken Fat

Like many other companies looking to enhance the flavor of their products, (at least back in those days) we would add fat. Chicken fat, that is. Fat is where the flavor is. If it were not, we would all be thinner.

Chicken fat is extremely slippery, rivaling the friction reducing properties of about any grease or oil. I can't imagine the mess they have extracting the fat from the chicken carcasses. Rather nasty, I would think.

Our chicken fat came to us in 5 gallon plastic buckets with lids on them. The buckets were stacked up on a pallet with a narrow band of reinforced tape around the top.

One day a guy on a forklift truck was moving the chicken fat into the raw materials cooler for use in the frozen foods department. They bumped into something. Most of the time, these stupid messes are avoidable. It happens when they do not look, or they force something without being able to see what they are doing, hoping that it will be okay. (I learned those lessons the hard way myself.)

It wouldn't be a big deal if a few buckets fell and popped open. This time, several stacks of the buckets fell over and popped open. To make matters worse, because of the cool air and floor in the cooler, the chicken fat was setting up like lard.

Den Warren

It was interesting to watch the cleanup crew trying to take care of this. They tried using hot water and flushing it down the drain. This really wasn't working. Fat floats on water, of course, and the volume of the mess kept getting bigger. Chicken fatty water was drifting under everything in the cooler. The entire cooler would need emptied and cleaned up real well. If they would have shoveled up the semi-solidified slush it would have worked out a lot better for them.

It was so incredibly slippery. No matter how careful they were, they could NOT keep their footing. They were slipping and falling into the slimy gunk. Certainly chickens would be laughing at them if it were possible.

I decided I would let them do their job and sit that one out. I knew I would be on the floor if I got involved. I just shook my head and went the other way.

Ladies Man: A crew leader working for me called me at home. He was desperate for advice. He had gotten two women pregnant at the same time. He was contemplating suicide. All I could think of was telling him he had to stay alive to support the babies. I don't know how it turned out.

Rancid Tales

Top Ten Messes; Mess #7

Dry Heaves

If you are eating right now, put your bookmark here and save this for later.

I worked as a supervisor at a plant that processed dairy products and gelatin desserts. For a big part of my time there, I was in charge of plant sanitation. My crew had a team leader and around 10 sanitors.

In food processing, there is a striking amount of waste. You wonder why you make the effort to clean your plate when you see the large volume of waste being generated. But there are reasons why the product cannot be packaged up and given away. There is packaging, labor, utilities, and shipping cost. Some product or ingredients are out of date. Sometimes an wrong ingredient is added or the wrong amount added that would make the ingredient statement false. The product may be contaminated, or suspected of being contaminated. On and on. . .

Back at our trash dock, we would dump 55 gallon barrels of waste chip dip, sour cream, and other such highly, highly perishable items into our trash compactor outside in whatever weather we were having.

The compactor sat down in a loading dock, so you did not have to raise up a barrel weighing hundreds of pounds to dump it. Basically, you just had to tip them over into the compactor. The dumping maneuver was not a problem. The compactor pushed the waste back into an empty dumpster.

Den Warren

The problem with the situation is that slop does not compact. It would rather just ooze out of the cracks or the side of the compactor, so it did, by the gallon each day. This accumulation was old, and . . .urp, rank. It was not often that we could clean the area, except around the outside of the compactor. Underneath was garbage HELL.

One day I was determined not to let the situation continue. When the dumpster got moved out, we were going to clean the asphalt. Everyone knew of my intention and they got incredibly busy.

This left just the team leader and myself. The team leader was a valuable worker and I really appreciated all of his help. He was not perfect, but it was easy to overlook his faults because he was always there when needed.

So we watched the dumpster being pulled away. It revealed a multicolored mass of waste about the same size and shape as the space underneath the huge dumpster. The blob was just plain noxious. The stink was a cartoonish, apocalyptic, wretched stink as if we were at the sphincter of the planet.

We did not have time to marvel at how this horrifying spectacle came to be. The waste management driver was waiting on us to do the job so he could put in a new hopper.

Generally, I do not have a problem with smelly stuff. I was still able to function. My team leader was not faring so well. I started joking about eating lunch and he started yacking and dry heaving, but he kept working. So I quit with the stupid jokes.

We had to shovel this cesspool of waste into barrels and hoist them back up to the dock so they could be re-dumped later in the next dumpster.

Other sanitors would come along and watch us. Maybe move a barrel or two and laugh and walk away, preferring better air to breathe.

It was horrible. We filled up about 20 barrels or so as full as we could, and still be able to lift them. Once this traumatic chore was done. (Note: This is making me sick to my stomach just thinking about this as I write.) Then we had to hose down the dock. I wanted it clean enough to eat off of. (Just kidding.}

We must have did a perfect job. It never needed done again.

Close Call: I was cleaning a dough mixer that would only run if the lid was down. I had a big metal belt buckle that touched the proximity sensor and briefly caused the mixer to run. it could have been badly hurt. I reported the situation and I was told to be more careful next time.

Den Warren

Mess #6

Fast Track to Insanity; Soup Line Revisited

As mentioned earlier, the soup line ran 400 cans per minute. If all went well, the cans would stream down the can track from the in-line cooker. At the end of the lengthy can track was the packing area. Workers there had the immense responsibility of running a corrugated case sealer.

Each box had 12 or 24 cans in it. If the cases were not gluing or closing properly, they had to be set aside and run when there was a gap in the line. At times stack upon stack of full, unsealed boxes were sitting off to the side on pallets.

If a case would jam in the machine, which was a common occurrence, the cans would accumulate on the conveyor.

Full cans of soup were moving at a high rate of speed down the track to accommodate the speed of the line. Whenever the line accumulated cans, or "backed up" the cans would smash together and leave dents.

If the line did not pack out cans for a few minutes, perhaps due to a mechanical problem, they would back all the way up to the cooker. It that happened, they would fall out into baskets. At 400 per minute, to would not take very long to fill a basket.

If cooker baskets were being filled, an immediate decision had to be made whether to stop the cooker. If the cooker was stopped, it had to be timed. If the time exceeded a certain amount, all of the thousands of cans in the cooker were overcooked and would have to be scrapped.

Also, if the cooker stopped, the canning area would have to stop since there was nowhere for them to go.

Cans going into the cooker were required to have a certain internal temperature for proper processing. So if they sat on the line too long waiting to go into the cooker they would also become no good.

Cans dented after the cooker could not be reprocessed because they would become mush the second time around. They could not be canned without being through the cooker because they would not be commercially sterile.

I found, as a quality Tech, this area to be a total running nightmare and desired to get away from it. There was no fun to be had there. The regular speed lines were bad enough. As a quality control technician, the line was an immense pain.

The only experience I had in the area as a production worker was to stack boxes on pallets for shipment. These boxes spewed out of the case sealer at the rate of over 30 boxes per minute, or one every two seconds. Don't stop to scratch anything.

I have done this job for 8 hour shifts. This was very demanding and hard on a worker's back as they barely had time to straighten themselves.

Eventually the case stacking later became automated.

Den Warren

Mess #5

Spiraling Out of Control

I was a second shift production supervisor in a frozen foods processing plant. My line was a frozen entrée line, items suitable for microwave preparation.

Product from our line went into a large spiral freezer. It functioned like a large escalator. The product in the packages would go onto the freezer conveyor, about a half dozen across, then would spiral in an upward direction inside of the freezer. They went up about 20 feet into the subzero air. Once the product got to the top, it would go onto another spiral that would spiral downward. Then the product would exit the freezer on the other side in the packout area.

It was about minus 20 degrees F in there, not counting the wind chill from the powerful fans. When the product came out, it would be frozen as hard as a rock. This process would take a couple of hours. Therefore, there were hundreds of packages, perhaps a couple thousand in the freezer at a time.

Someone form the Research and Development Department wanted to do a study on filling volumes in certain packages, then freeze them. They just used water for the study because it cost nothing.

Second shift got stuck doing all of their work for them. We had some operators filling water into trays and packaging them. Then into the freezer. This activity was a mere sideshow to all of the other problems that were going on. The study did not warrant much attention.

Later in the shift, the crew leader from the packaging department told me that the test packages were stuck and would not come out of the freezer. This made no sense at all.

I went over there and tried to pull them out. You could beat the ice cubes all you wanted and they would not fit out of the exit. The exit conveyor was under the packages as well as over them.

"Oh no!" I realized that they were filled with water. Water expands when you freeze it.

Sure enough. I opened up the freezer and gazed upon the horrific scenario. We were not going to be able to unload anything in the freezer. It was all frozen and expanded too big to run out! Production was supposed to run after the test but we were dead in the water with the icy mess for the rest of the shift and into the next shift.

Immediately I turned off the cooling to the freezer and opened up what doors I could. There I was, mostly by myself since we were always short-handed. I was frantically trying to bust up the thawing stubborn packages on the spirals while freezing rain from the ill-conceived test packages came drizzling down on me.

Bash awhile, then spin the spiral a bit and get at some more product where we could reach it. My job typically made me work about seven days a week, almost every week. I worked 5 hours or so overtime that night trying to straighten out the mess. I was not happy. At all.

This situation made me think about who should have been there helping me.   Those individuals did not work at all during any weekend. At least my fury helped me have the vigor to extract the packages.

My effort devoted to recovering the cataclysmic mess was pretty much disregarded by production management as a non-event.

Watch This. . .

We were all crazy about pro football. We knew every person's favorite team at the company. We would taunt each other every time we met if they were from an opposing faction. The most zealous factions were the Browns, Steelers, and Cowboy fans.

One day one of the guys was selling team watches at the company. They were very popular. They were only $5 each. A pretty good deal, we figured. But I doubt if any of them ran very long.

Anyway, one of the Browns fans was among the first to get a watch. He also bought a Steelers watch. I saw him go up to a Steelers fan and show it to him.

The Steelers fan was covetous of the brand new Steelers watch. The Browns fan let the Steelers fan get all wrapped up into looking at the timepiece. Then he slammed it on the floor and stomped on it a couple of times! It was stupid funny.

In reality, the Browns fan probably got more satisfaction out of his purchase than any of the rest of us. Steelers suck.

Den Warren

Mess #4

It's Raining Soy Sauce

When product came off of the line it was put into cases. The cases were stacked on wooden pallets. The pallets with full cases of product on them were about five feet high each. They were then stretch wrapped with clear plastic.

Out in our shipping warehouse, there were tall racks where the loads were placed into with a forklift. The racks were up to four loads high.

From personal experience, I can tell you that going four pallets high on the racks with a heavy load is touchy. It requires full attention. The worst thing I ever put up four high was a load of four 55 gallon barrels of soy sauce concentrate. That product is a lot denser that water. With all of that weight, going all that high, it felt like the back end of the forklift was wanting to lift up off of the floor.

I have picked up very heavy loads with the forklift. If you exceed the lifting capacity, the back end will come up off of the floor, then you have no steering since the steering is in the back. You could tip over. That adds extra concern to the job.

The first time I ever drove a forklift, my department manager told me to get on the forklift and do the job. I did not want to, with the high potential for damage and injury. A forklift is much heavier than a car. Food plants are extremely crowded and there is always something or someone in the way.

Nevertheless, they made me drive the forklift with no training whatsoever. The first time I got on one and moved it, I back up and broke a light off of it. They just laughed it off and said to keep going.

I drove forklift quit a lot over the years. The key is to assume nothing. Look everywhere all of the time.

Anyway, I was out in the warehouse looking for some packaging, I think. A forklift driver was walking around in a daze with the shift manager. He had tried to put up a full load of bottled soy sauce on the top level. Evidently the load caught something and the stretch wrapping broke and cases fell like cluster bombs from the height down on him.

Fortunately for the driver, there was a roll cage on top of him. No full cases could hit him.

However, that did not stop him from being battered with shattering glass bottles that broke upon impact of hitting the roll cage. A salvo of hundreds of full bottles barraged him as they fell from the warehouse stratosphere. Most of the load had fallen.

To add insult to injury the salty soy sauce drenched the cuts to his body. You never know how many cuts and blemishes you have on your body until you are drenched with soy sauce and feel them all burn.

One time I was hooking together a hose from a pump and it burst open. I was drenched. Completely. I had little stings everywhere. Of course that minor discomfort was not as bad as bringing attention to myself by looking like a walking piece of chicken teriyaki.

The mess from the costly bottled soy sauce mess was huge. You can imagine the mess in your kitchen at home if you would break one bottle of soy sauce.

Puddles of soy sauce ran and glass bounced all over the area. There were piles of wicked broken glass to clean up. Many load of finished product had to be moved and cleaned under.

The supervisor made the driver clean it up. I had to take his place so he could do it. My job at the time was to run a crew who packed special order institutional sized frozen packages. No one took my place, but my crew was responsible and well trained. I was just glad I did not have to clean up that one.

Mess #3

Pizza Room Problems

One of the food plants I worked at had three pizza assembly rooms. One of the rooms was a high speed pizza operation. I was the supervisor of that room on second shift.

This was a very difficult operation to manage. It has been said, and I think rightly so, that if you can supervise in the food industry, you can supervise anywhere.

However, just because you can do something does not mean that you want to. I hated every single day working there with a passion without exception. They paid me very well to relocate there so I figured I owed them a year of service. Further, it doesn't look good on your resume to change companies that frequently.

Every day I would go into this Stephen King deli of a pizza room and look at our orders. We would change over 20 or more times a day, with almost no stopping. Then I would make the production schedule for our room.

First the orders had to be organized by the type of pizza sauce. The sauce was the most time-consuming thing to change. One store-brand customer had to have their own. Unfortunately for us, it was really tasty and was not going to ever be changed to our regular sauce. Nor would they allow the other brands to use their sauce. (Admittedly many years later I still go out to one of their stores and buy their pizzas from time to time.)

Den Warren

Next, I would arrange the orders by crust size. The crust was very demanding to manage. I wore a radio and had to call for crust size changes from the bakery, which came into our room non-stop via a direct conveyor.

I had to coordinate the correct crust size to come on the conveyor at the correct time for each order. If we did not have the crust come into the room at the correct time, we had to stack off crusts and have downtime, or send someone over to the bakery to pick up some more crusts of the size we needed until the correct size arrived by conveyor. The wrong sized crusts had to be continually stacked off.

I also had to manage the toppings. I tried to delegate this to a line person and he did a pretty good job of it. Sometimes I had to intervene. If the topping room could not supply us, we actually had to make on-the-fly real time complicated changes to the schedule and coordinate the aforementioned all over again.

Then we had to put the correct brand label on each pizza. We had our own labels for our own brand, then some of the customers wanted their own store label put on them.

To make it all that much worse, customers wanted us to put idiotic price tags on their pizzas. Most of the time, the tag was not the real price, but an inflated price to make the real price look low.

Owners of food companies love to be the direct salesmen and sell the product without worrying about how to make it all. Evidently they find the production side of things a nuisance. Our management was more than happy to oblige with the price tags. They tell the customers they can have whatever they want.

Another such owner of a place I supervised had over 900 SKU (Shelf Keeping Units) In other words, by the time you added all the various store brands and sizes, there were over 900 products.

The only problem with such "service" is that the stress of it ruins their own people's health and destroys their families. At one such location I personally knew an employee who routinely worked mandatory 16 hour plus days. (up to at least 19 hours) He dropped dead while working on the line.

I am not the person someone wants to talk to if they are a big advocate of JIT (Just In Time)   While they talk about the philosophy of it, I have seen the ugly reality of it.

This low inventory madness has ruined about every job in the country. It creates total perpetual chaos. It bets that things will go perfectly, and of course they don't. The steep costs of this ideal is not readily evident on paper.

I digress even further; There was a clothing store in my hometown. They had been in business for a few generations. The clothing store was way too big for the small town, but customers came there from all over.

I asked the owner of the clothing store one time how he attracted business from other towns. He said that when times are tough, they would increase their inventory and selection, while all the other stores would cut back to save money. The store was out of business not long after it was bought by a younger couple who went in a different direction.

The pizza room was so accommodating to the customer with its nearly unlimited amount of options. Everything was custom order. This had a huge cost in changeovers, confusion, waste, and definitely misery.

Note that this "customer" is not the consumer, but a middleman.

The misery of high turnover manifests itself in hiring and training costs, which are huge when you factor in all of the mistakes a new person makes. These costs don't readily show up anywhere on the income statement.

The store chains loved the ridiculous price stickers. Sadly this stupid and deceptive practice was usually not even the real price. Retail chains would have us put them on. Then once they got to the store, they would put on a lower price with their own sticker to make it look like a discount. This marketing practice added a whole layer of complexity to managing the already unwieldy, broken production system.

Sometimes an order would only run about 5 minutes. We would scramble to get the exact amount of pizzas in the last few boxes and have to be ready to go to the next order. What brand? What price? Etc.

Sometimes, during the confusion too many cases of an order would be made up. So among our other duties, we would have to take all the labels off of the pizzas and repack then again with the correct one.

After making the schedule, it would be time for the workers to arrive. I would take into account who was absent. The low-wage people miss a lot of work because their lives are in constant turmoil. They get "hurt" a lot. Their quality is often suspect. Their comprehension of anything complex is often weak. There are always just enough of the good ones there to keep the doors open. The good ones must be treated like gold.

Another major difficulty in the multi-faceted mess is the wrapping machine. It puts the layer of clear plastic over the pizzas.

While packaging, if we would find holes bigger than a millimeter on the back of the cardboard along the seam, we would have to unwrap the pizzas. While unwrapping them, pepperoni slices or other toppings would stick to the plastic and go flying off.

Stopping the line and feeding these pizzas back through the wrapper again was a big downtime problem.

One time a USDA inspector came in and opened a twin pack of pizzas and found a pepperoni missing. Our pepperoni slicing machine was pretty good, but not infallible. Our inspection on the line was quite fallible as well.

Since this one pizza was not fully topped by one slice, it was considered underweight by the Federal Government. We had to go through and re-open pallets loaded with cases of twin-packs. We had to open and inspect every pizza for any missing pepperonis. Then we had to replace everything that fell off. We did not have good production numbers that night.

When I first started at the company, the room was a total disaster. People would wander away from the room. I caught one guy laying down in the break room in the bakery. The pizza room had a ridiculous amount of downtime. The monkeys were clearly running the zoo.

Immediately we started doing better. There was nowhere to go but up. This progress continued through the weeks and months that followed. I worked hard with the people who were used to doing things their own way, to assemble a better team.

Those who did not want to get with the program would be weeded out. Sometimes I would get people in the room who were too good for the job (literally) and should have been making more money working somewhere else. I treated them with respect and gave them more important responsibilities. They would either stay awhile longer or get promoted and be more long term.

Another issue in dealing with the chaotic room was getting the line to stop when things started to get out of control. They would pile up unwrapped pizzas at the wrapper. They would pile up pizzas without toppings at the topping machine. They were piled way up to be packed. Stacked pizzas would look terrible if they sat there for long.

I couldn't figure out why they would stack stuff up and not stop. They agreed that they wanted to not have to work around stacks of pizzas. But then they still kept doing it. Finally, I realized they were previously often yelled at by my boss, Priscilla. Priscilla yelled at people not to stop the line.

From what she told me, Priscilla thought I could be a good tyrant like her. Maybe she thought I would go into the room and forcibly whip everyone into shape and make her look like the fantastic manager that she was not.

As I mentioned, I hated every single day I worked there with a passion. To be fair, much of it was Priscilla's doing. She was far from qualified to be my boss. On a personal level, she was difficult to work with. She would talk down to everyone like they were a child. She had a negative opinion of black people. Her only management experience was evidently rooted in being a mom.

I totally disagreed with her way of doing things. She did nothing but add to the chaos and waste. She did not come into the room much, at my request, but when she did, all she did was come in there and yell around at my people awhile and make them stack up pizzas. When she would leave, I would immediately stop and bring the situation back to a sensible working condition.

In her simple mind, she expected us to never have problems with the entire mess I have described here. When we did, she would try to blame me by saying, "You had a really rough night last night." Of course we did. We always did. Then she would come up with her simplistic solutions such as , "You have to keep the lines running and don't let them stop all the time." It was like I was supposed to prevent the problems by yelling at the people. The supervisors who yelled at the people in the other pizza rooms were held in high esteem at the Company by their "coordinators".

One Afternoon, Priscilla decided that she needed to personally intervene after one of these "rough nights". She came into the room for an extended period of time and was yelling at my people for not doing things her chaotic way. Her yelling came across to them as for no good reason and contemptuous. People started asking me to get her out of the room. I knew they were right. She wasn't helping anything.

So I did just that. I asked her to let me run the room. This is what I was there for. She insinuated that I was incompetent. I did not have all of the "experience" that she had. In my mind, I was under-hired and should have been her boss.

Therefore I requested a private meeting with her. I basically told her I disagreed with her way of doing things and that her expectations were unreasonable. She stood up and glared at me, in contempt, and told me nothing. Very unprofessional, I thought.

Then she went and got her boss the production manager, Mr. Poindexter. Poindexter swallowed Priscilla's version of what was going on without even listening to me. Poindexter had almost never even set foot into my room. He was a little guy who wanted to show me who was boss, I guess. That surprised me, because I thought he was a lot smarter than that.

Poindexter told me that he was moving me temporarily into one of the slow rooms. This was supposedly my degrading punishment for my belligerent display of trying to talk to my boss. I was elated to get away from her nonsense.

That job in the slow room was such cake. I did not mind it at all. No tension, no chaos. It seemed to me I could be quite content to stay there.

But after only a week or so, Priscilla came into the room and asked me if I was ready to come back to her room.

I flatly told her, "no."

To my astonishment, she said, "I can't believe you said that."

Why would I want to go back to her torment?

The guy who replaced me for a week in the high speed room was a big time yeller. I understood it because he didn't know any other way. So we did get along okay.

He wanted out of there badly. He pleaded with the managers. He told them how tough it was in there and how bad he wanted out.

At least some of my people wanted me back. Poindexter put me back, rationalizing that I had learned my "lesson", even though I never dropped the contention that they were always totally off-base.

Due to the brevity of my stay in the slow room, I felt that their quick reversal gave me righteous leverage over my cowardly detractors.

As an epilogue to all this pizza pain; the next company I went to also hired Poindexter. Awhile after I was there. I knew he was going to be a problem for me there. Sure enough, Poindexter still had the idea I was a troublemaker. My co-workers at the new company wondered what his problem was. I suspect Poindexter and Priscilla submarined me later in my goofy career by giving me some bad references.

I resolved that I would never tolerate anyone like them again. Ever.

Den Warren

The Phantom Wrestler

Perhaps he heard of my wrestling loss to Armando (from Canadian Adventure) or because he was bigger than me, Cleon was bragging that he could beat me in a wrestling bout. I asked him if he ever had any wrestling training, and he told me he hadn't.

I told him there was no chance he would beat me. He said he could with no problem, so I challenged him.

When I was involved in High School wrestling, once in awhile someone would think it was easier than it looked, and they were big and bad, so they came into the practice room to challenge us. It was barely worth our attention. We knew that our smallest guy could take anyone who wandered in. So I was basically assured of a victory, and I gave Cleon no satisfaction at all. So we agreed to meet at a town park after work for the match.

Word of the match spread like wildfire. When I got to the park it was closed. Cars from work were pouring into the park to see the action. I thought for sure we were going to get busted, but I was not going to be the one who backed down from the challenge.

We waited for awhile and no Cleon. We wondered, what was taking him so long? A guy from another area of the plant was there. He went to the nearby bar and found Cleon sitting there drinking. Cleon told the guy that he guessed he fooled us all.

I proclaimed victory by default and got out of there before the police came. A disappointed crowd badgered Cleon hard while he was at work the next day.

I reminded him that the challenge was still open. He never took me up on it. Wimp.

Mess #2

Fifty Pound Biscuits

One day I arrived at work to find that the entire plant had been shut down. There had been a fire in a flour bin that was at least 30 feet tall. A level detector inside the bin had shorted out caused the dusty contents of the bin to catch on fire.

The flour bin was in my area at the time. So another worker and I had the unenviable assignment of removing the burnt contents of the massive bin so the level detector could be worked on. The flour was black and brown and still had hot sparks intermingled with it. The smell was bad. The flour had baked into massive chunks so large that they had to be broken up by force just to get them through the man door to the bin.

This was perhaps the most physically demanding night of work that I have ever been involved with. The dust and heat was terrible.

All the while we were doing this, other than a few people hauling the biscuits to the scrap, everyone else was sitting around in the safety of the break room. You'd think the bosses would get the idea to swap us out occasionally.

Den Warren

Secret Conversations

I have worked with a lot of unusual people over the years. Perhaps Phil was the weirdest of them all. Phil had a couple of different jobs during the time I worked with him. One of the jobs was to mix dough for egg rolls. All he had to do was sit there and let the machine automatically add flour and automatically add water. If the mixture was too wet or dry, it would quickly be adjusted manually by adding flour or water.

Simple as this was, Phil would always end up in a panic because of his wonky work habits. He would be sitting there staring out into space. Then he would start mumbling. The he would start talking to himself. Then he would start pacing the floor and yelling an flailing his arms wildly in a fit of rage.

We would try to call out to him while this was going on. He was a nice guy. He would smile and then enhance his mellow. But then after a short period of time, would go through the same process. He would simmer for awhile. Next thing you knew he would be right back to the outbursts.

Phil was weird in some other ways too. I saw him grab a whole wedge of cheese once from a carry in luncheon and scoop up half a container of chip dip with it and cram the whole thing into his mouth. He had some other detestable habits that I will not go into here.

Phil would scream at his real or imagined adversaries while he would pacing back and forth in front of the dough mixer. While this show was taking place, the dough would become unusable. Then Phil would finally realize things were out of kilter, so he would panic and either pour a ridiculous amount of water into the mixer or go berserk shoving a stupid amount of flour into the mixer. Flour would be flying everywhere as he hastily tried to recover the mixer.

When we saw the action, we knew we would soon be getting a break from making the egg roll filling as the line would be down and the crew leader would be there to chew him out. Phil really had the knack of making the simplest job look difficult.

We always wondered what he was talking about during his solitaire arguments. We heard that he was re-enacting his divorce court. The guy I worked directly with started sneaking up on him while the drama was going on to eavesdrop. He would get close, then Phil would always catch him sneaking up. It was fun to watch because Phil was a good sport about it and would feign anger.

Den Warren

Mess #1

Fryer Fire

One of my jobs was to change filters for our in-line noodle fryer. I did this on second shift.

Hundreds of gallons of hot 350 degree Fahrenheit oil would circulate through the large fryer. If the fryer would become plugged up from not being changed in a timely manner, the product in the fryer would ignite an cause a fire. The filters were to be changed every 25 minutes or so.

I professed that the fire would never happen to me and it didn't.

The day shift operator liked to put off doing the changes because he hoped I would come in and take care of his filters. I complained about it but nothing ever got done, since I covered their negligence.

One day this practice caught up with them. The product in the fryer ignited right at the end of the shift. The fire spread outside of the hot oil in the fryer. The room was built with porous concrete and fryer oil soaked its way into everything. The hot fire spread to electric wires, ceiling tiles, everything was engulfed.

I had just got there and we were scurrying about looking for fire extinguishers to pour onto the spreading fire until the fire department got there. No one was hurt, but things were burned so badly that the room was down for about a week. After business as usual returned, there was no change in the way day shift did their filter changing.

19 September 1979

The Ride Home

My car was in the shop. My boss, Rocky, consented to bringing me home, even though I found out later my place was not anywhere near on his way home.

Rocky has done some interesting things. He was the Pastor of a church for awhile. He played guitar while he and his wife sang at Jerry Falwell's church on television once.

Rocky has a keen interest in the spiritual welfare of people. He took such an interest in me as well. He asked me if I knew I would go to Heaven when I died. I told him I did not. He simply showed me that Jesus promises in the Bible that he will save whoever calls upon him. (But you have to ask.) I was very interested in what he said. One verse reads that "In hope of eternal life, which God, that cannot lie, promised before the world began." (Titus 1:2) God would have no reason to lie. I chose with an open mind to accept what he said in the Bible as truth.

I have often let God down since then. He has never let me down, and never will. Do yourself a favor and consider the truth of God's Bible if you haven't already.

Den Warren

Twister

I was on my usual five mile afternoon drive through the countryside on the way to work. The weather did not seem threatening at all, although it was a little dark out. I glanced over to the north and saw a Tornado!

When I was a child I was very close to a tornado that did a lot of damage to our town. Also we saw damage from other tornadoes in the area. My fear of tornadoes was not too irrational, but I had a very healthy respect for them.

The location where I spotted the tornado was near my parent's house so I stopped and told my Dad, who was sleeping because he worked third shift.

I told him, "Hey! Get up! There's a tornado outside!" I suppose all tornadoes are outside.

"No there's not." He was a little groggy.

"Yes there is! Look outside!"

He looked out the window and saw it. "There is!"

Then I tried to call home, since my wife and two children were swimming outside when I left only a couple miles away. No one answered the phone. Here they were, outside swimming while a tornado lurked so close to them. What if lightning hit them?

So I went back outside trying to figure out what to do next. We watched it. And watched it. It was probably about as small as they get. It was about three quarters of a mile away, or about a kilometer away.

It went up and down like a yo-yo. Boards and small items were being picked up by it and flying around in it. We continued to watch it. Okaaaaay. . .We became less excited as we watched.

So I told Dad I might as well go to work. On the way there I kept my eye on the phenomenon. it was running parallel path with me to work. I watched it travel the whole way with me, all the while staying low to the ground and keeping its full funnel form. Very weird.

By the time I got to work I was desensitized to the thing. I casually walked into the HR office and told the manager that there was a tornado nearby.

"What?! Don't come in here and tell me that!"

I invited him to go outside and look. We both went outside. Naturally, it was nowhere to be seen. The weather still did not look threatening, which made my assertion all the more unbelievable.

Fortunately, someone had reported the funnel to a local paper the next day to confirm my claim and salvage my credibility.

I would still recommend keeping your distance from any tornado if you suspect one is near. All it would take is an object to slam into you to ruin your whole day.

Den Warren

All Engineers are NOT Jerks

It is very difficult to face this fact. I am not saying that just because someone is an engineer they are not a jerk. Not at all. Occasionally you will find a pretty cool one. What I am saying is that just because someone has chosen the field of engineering, it does not automatically mean they are a jerk.

Granted, you may know engineers who are jerks. I know some engineers who have intolerable behavior; know it all; belligerent; defensive; and generally have no clue about how to carry on a normal conversation without being the center of attention, or somehow better than whoever they are talking to.

I knew an engineer who could not talk without trying to be a smartass. His comments were not witty, just pathetic. I always regretted speaking to the guy. You wonder how a guy like that could have any friends. If they have any, they are probably engineers.

Engineers do have people who they can work with. . .other engineers. When engineers are working together, there is this competition among them to see who knows the most. In other areas, people are generally happy to be surrounded by competent people.

How do people choose the engineering profession? Either they got beaten up a lot, or were the ones doing the beating. At any rate their dads would probably not talk to them much unless they were building something fabulous. Jerks will never be successful being a salesman or a supervisor because they have to work closely with people.

Any person who is young and a jerk should first try not t be a jerk. If they cannot change, they should go into something that limits their exposure to the rest of us meaningless carbon units. They would be better off working with things, not people. Young jerk, be an engineer.

Package Identification

Most people are not aware of the meanings of certain symbols on food packages.

A "U" with a circle around it means the product is approved as kosher by the Orthodox Union.

You can also tell what company makes a product for a private store label, at least if it has meat as an ingredient. On the top of the can or package, you will see a code starting with "EST" or "P". This establishment or poultry number identifies the plant it was processed in for tracking purposes. If you look on the USDA website for the numbers that follow after that on the package, you can see what plant the product was packaged in.

Den Warren

Wild Animals

The most physically demanding regular job I have ever done was shoveling 110 pounds of bean sprouts into a plastic barrel on a scale every 30 seconds, then with a helper, dumping the barrel into a hopper. This was an all day job that someone had to do every day. I have done it a number of times myself. It was grueling, boring, and a real killer.

There were two guys on day shift who had this job as their regular job. These guys were wild-eyed knuckle-dragging maniacs. The way they acted made you think they had to be on something. But to their credit, they did an awesome job of keeping all the sensible people off of the torment.

There was a drawback to having those guys over there. They were insane. While they were working they performed monkey-like antics. One time one of them yanked the other one's pants down while they were working. Intended or not, the underwear dropped down too. The audience for that one included some women.

They never got into trouble for that, since no one made an issue out of anything that they did. One day one of them grabbed the other one an hoisted him overhead, which had to be at full arm's length, and threw him into the mung bean sprout trough. This was a huge operation that was like an indoor creek.

This time they did get into trouble. They had gone too far. with safety being at stake.

I was not a main player in determining their fate, but I did put in my own two cents. I expressed that you cannot have a job suitable for a pack animal, then expect a noble gentry to do it.

I don't know if I had any influence, but they did stay on the job, probably with a write up and a stern warning, resulting in them dialing it down a little.

Sometime after that, I heard that the job finally had become automated.

Coveting: A guy was telling another guy out in the warehouse how bad he wanted to get with a woman, he mentioned her name and what he wanted to do with her in graphic detail. He didn't know it, but the guy he was talking to was her husband.

Den Warren

Harold's Bloody Rampage

When packaging frozen meals, care must be taken that each package is sealed all the way around. We had someone check each package. They checked them by tapping on each package firmly as it came down the line before it went into the freezer.

By touching the package on the center of the lid, if there is an unsealed segment, the lid would collapse as air was pushed out of the package. They would do about one package per second, all day long.

I tried to explain to the engineering staff there how we utilized a "tapper" device at another company. The tapper would pick up that a package was approaching the station with an electric eye, then a rod would come down and tap it like an operator's finger. If the tapper travelled too far down, the a puff of compressed air would blow the package off of the conveyor.

Since we were blessed with cheap labor willing to do mindless jobs seven days a week, we used humans to do the tapping.

It was really a frustration, that the workers thought I didn't know anything since I was the new guy at the Company. On the other hand, I was the first one to implement production downtime sheets with that Company. I am not bragging that this was a major accomplishment. It would be the equivalent of bringing matches to a primitive tribe in Brazil.

The production supervisors were constantly being beat down for the actions and poor written communication, which was written out in slop longhand on note paper. They turned in this pile of drivel every day to the tyrannical management who threw fits about everything on the journals and everything that was not in the pathetic journals.

Anyway, if a small noodle or something was on the package's seal area, the lid would not seal. This was a big problem with fettuccine, being a very long noodle that wanted to hang out of the sides.

If there was a lot of resealing to do, sometimes we would have to stop and catch them up. It was very annoying to have to stop, because production numbers were so vital. If we did not make the numbers, we would have to work on Saturday and usually Sunday as well.

The packages that did not seal could be re-sealed. We had an off-line sealer. If we cleaned any sauce off of the seal area they could be resealed on the off-line re-sealer without having to stop and feed them back into the line. The lids were manufactured with their own adhesive, so our equipment had to heat up the seal area, then press the lid and tray together.

On one occasion, there was too much resealing to do, so we had to stop running the line and feed them back through. While the crew was working on the re-sealing, under the watchful eye of their crew leader, Mike, I took the opportunity to go do some paperwork.

Mike came storming into the office, "Harold got his hand in the re-sealer and is running around getting blood all over everything!"

"Stop him!"

"I can't"

So I went out there, wondering what horrific scenario I was walking into. Since this happened to Harold, that meant that he had to have his hand in the sealer while he activated it with the foot pedal. His hand was cut severely and also burned badly by the seal bar.

Sure enough, the goof was still pacing quickly all over the place, holding his injured hand with the other one at the wrist and shaking it about, spraying blood all over the place. People were watching in horror.

I have been hurt before. So have you. Tell me that this guy was not stupid for the way he was acting.

I cornered him and led him away from the line. I instructed the crew leader to completely clean the area and scrap all of the product in the area. He was great and did a nice job of it.

A person ought to have some compassion for the injured. But I have to admit that this was very difficult for me under the circumstances. The plant was in a rural town with the hospital quite a distance away.

Rancid Tales

Once at the hospital, there was quite possibly a very long wait there for treatment. Naturally, there was no one else to run these people over there.

One time when it was early on second shift, I asked the HR manager if he could do a hospital run so I could manage my operation. He was very insulting and rude with me. They wanted nothing whatsoever to do with interacting with the people.

As a supervisor, when you got back from the hospital, you could expect quite a bit of unwanted, unpaid overtime to make up for the time lost caused by the distraction. Never would you be thanked by anyone for any part of it.

Then I had the privilege of adding insult to Harold's injury by presenting him with a write-up for unsafe behavior. Harold did not loses any fingers, and he made an excellent tapper for a long time afterwards.

FOOD PLANT SUPERVISORS: Would all appreciate reading these Rancid Tales. If you any know Food Production People, why not get them a copy?

Den Warren

Ergonomic Challenge

We had a very good crew in the frozen foods area of our food processing plant. I managed the packaging area at the time. We packaged oriental style entrées into trays, and each tray went into its own box. After the box was sealed, they made the journey down a rather lengthy conveyor belt up to a plate freezer.

When the boxes got to the end of the conveyor, and accumulated about six or so boxes, a pusher would slide the whole row into the plate freezer.

The freezer had stacks of huge metal plates that would go up or down. Once a plate was full of packages, the plate would automatically move to the next plate. While hot packages were going in, frozen ones would slid out the back.

One problem with this system was leaking boxes. If a box leaked, it would freeze fast to the plate. So if a hot box went up against the frozen box that was stuck, it would just smash and freeze there also.

Someone would have to go up the platform and try and dig out with long metal poles, all of the frozen blocks of meals that were stuck to the plate and each other.

After all of the digging and scraping, there could not be any chunks stuck to a plate of the chain wreck would start all over again.

Because of the ongoing battle with the plate freezer, it seemed that we always had someone stationed up there to get the jams out. Otherwise, the conveyor going up there would back up full of boxes and shut the line down.

If the conveyor backed up with boxes the force on them became great enough to smash them into each other. We did not want them to go into the freezer because they were already leaking.

One day we were runny pretty well. Not a lot of trouble with the freezer. I noticed the line was backing up but didn't worry about it too much because we had Beth up there.

Beth was one of my best workers. She could always be counted on to do a great job.

"Dang!" The belt was still filling up and looked like it was going to back all the way up, so I went up there.

Beth was looking at the problem kind of stupefied and not doing anything about it. Normally, this would have made me a little irate, but I couldn't recall her ever being up there before, so maybe she needed some further training. There was no way I was going to make one of my blue chips mad.

"Is there some kind of problem up here, Beth?"

She hesitated.

I asked, "Is there something you need help with here?"

"I can't do this."

"Really, how come?" The silence went on for awhile, and it gave me a really weird feeling. The line was down, so I had to ask, "Why can't you do this?"

She moved toward the plate freezer and stretched her arms forward. "I can't reach the packages."

"Why not? . . .Oooooh."

This demonstration helped me connect the dots. There was a bar across the pusher that you had to either reach over or under, which made the job much worse. But for Beth, that bar was right at Boob level, and she had loads of boobage. It would have been a real exercise in contortion for her to do that job, if at all. She had been quiet about the whole thing and did not know what to do since she did not want to bring the situation to anyone's attention.

No one had heard of the word "ergonomics" in those days, but clearly this situation was an ergonomic challenge. Seeing that Beth lacked the physical attributes (or had too much of them) to work at this station, I quietly switched her out of the job with someone else.

I made the excuse to the others that the freezer was bothering her. The excuse did not make her look too bad, because it would piss off everyone. However, my doing that was probably just another one of those things that make people think their boss is stupid for letting her get away with not doing it.

$100 Tirade

A high percentage of big dogs at companies feel it is their place to rule by intimidation and fear. They have no other tools in their tool pouch other than to walk around with a scowl on their face and complain incessantly. They dare not praise a worker for something, or the worker might think it is okay to become complacent.

No one was better at totalitarian management than the owner of one of the companies I worked for. This man started at least two very large food processing companies.

Since the owner was such a pain, naturally, some of those under him took the same approach as he was their role model. He liked to hire cronies and family members as top management, so they had no other example of how to run anything. You might say that he was a type of community organizer of sorts.

These lightweights that he set up with cushy jobs, had them at everyone else's expense. They were difficult to work with and had very little to offer the Company.

As proof of this entrepreneur's tyranny, he was featured on the television shows, *60 Minutes*, and *The Tonight Show*. He talked about how abusive he was to suppliers. He left out the part about how crappy he was to his own people.

I talked to one of his ex-COOs who was in charge of another company I worked for, and he told me that most of the drama was an act so he could get his way with people.

He would fire a supervisor for the least offense. He would fire them for putting salt on the food at a taste panel, since they were not getting the true flavor of what was being produced. I know that part was no act. He fired so many that his minions would hire them back later hoping that he would not realize it.

You would think that the owner of a large company would come strutting through the front door and expect the red carpet treatment. Not him.

Instead, he would have his limo driver take him around to the back of the plant. Then he would go into the trash dock and start going through the trash. He wanted to see what was being wasted.

At least one time he was so angry that he went from the trash dock to the production area. He used a lighter and lit a $100 bill and threw it down on the floor and stomped on it. Then he said, "You are wasting my money, so I might as well too!"

The clever little devil probably easily got his $100 worth of savings from his display.

I only saw the guy once. Our managers would not even let supervisors meet him, which I took offense at. However, maybe they were protecting us.

Winner Winner; Chicken Dinner

Evelyn was a worker at one of the places I was a supervisor at. She was a real problem child as we would describe those of her ilk.

A common trait of those sort of people is that they miss a lot of work. Evelyn missed a crazy amount. The usual protocol is that we interview people when their absenteeism reaches certain benchmarks, then give them write-ups of increasingly negative consequence.

We had so much absenteeism that some supervisors would try and ignore the problem because they were desperate not to lose the person. As difficult as it was to manage in food production situations, it was much more difficult to run short-handed. If someone did get fired, it would take a long time to get a replacement.

Human Resources was always trying to blame supervisors for being mean to people and running off their eminently qualified darlings that they hired.

Anyway, I had to bring Evelyn into the office for her absenteeism and her lack of personal hygiene. Her immediate team leader, another woman, had to be there as well. In the midst of the discussion, Evelyn started to go into graphic detail of her big bad menstrual period she was having.

Den Warren

    The team leader had an incredible ability to express herself with her eyebrows. The eyebrows were really working while Evelyn was brining up all of this unwanted information.

    It was really comical to see since Evelyn was oblivious to the crazy faces being made next to her. After the meeting, the team leader told me she could not believe that I did not react to any of the nasty information.

    Evelyn seemed to always have troublesome coincidences that she had no control over. One day another woman had her coat come up missing. Strangely enough, Evelyn had the same style and color of coat, but it was way too big for her.

    The coat's true owner was furious. She said that Evelyn stinks and did not want the coat back.

    I told Evelyn that I thought she was lying and she better not take anything else.

    On another occasion, the woman who had her coat stolen by Evelyn said the her chicken dinner was also stolen by Evelyn. She told me it was a fried chicken meal and that she we in the women's restroom eating it while in the stall.

    I waited outside for her. When she came out, I confronted her about it. Naturally, she said that she brought the same thing to eat that day. I told her that I did not believe her and that even if she was telling the truth, we did not want people to work here who thought it was okay to eat lunch in a restroom stall. I told her to go home. No one missed her.

Organoleptic Sampling

"Organo-what?" you ask. Every industry has to have a few terms to make themselves feel smart. Usually, as in this case, it is a complex word to describe something simple.

Organoleptic means is to smell and taste, and to feel texture in the mouth. That is what we had to do in the food lab. Often, I thought of it a lunch. This practice varied from company to company. At one place it was only on an as-needed basis. Another place, everything we ran was set out in quantity in a taste panel at the start of the shift.

At one company we had to taste the food every two hours. There were numerous items to try and the food was really good. I went home full every day, which was usually seven days a week. Since it was like a buffet every two hours we had no use for taking a lunch.

What was amazing to me is that the higher someone ranked in the company, all companies, the more able they were to distinguish nuances in the food. Incredibly, those who worked under them were always able to notice the same thing once it was brought to their attention. They would ask me if I tasted whatever it was that they tasted, I would usually flatly say, "No," because it just wasn't there for me.

They actually had seminars for quality control people to practice tasting foreign matter in food. For instance, they would taste food grade (edible) machine grease and food grade machine oil. This grease and oil was not the type that you would use in your frying pan, but what was used the lube the machinery. This was done because there was a chance that the lubes could drip down into some food.

It saved a big controversy one time when I tasted foreign matter that fell into a batch. By comparison I was able to determine that it was the food grade grease.

The globs of grease had apparently ran off of a bearing. That kept us from putting tons of food on hold or scrapping it.

How I Learned to Complain: My first job ever was to shovel celery half the time, Which was extremely grueling work. No woman could do it. Period.

After the shoveling, the rest of the time was spent watching celery fill the tanks on the other end of the pipe. I wondered why I kept shoveling and not watching.

My female crew leader informed me that the other guy told her I didn't want to switch.

"What!?", I told her, "Why would anyone want to do that job. If you would have ever done the job for any time at all, you would have had more sense than to believe that!"

Space Trek: The Second Shift

For over 25 of my working years, I was on second shift. So I have a great deal of empathy for those who work on the off shifts. The off shifts generally outperform day shift, even though day shift has all of the extra management and technical "help" running around. Maybe that is the problem.

But I always figured that day shift people were low energy and bitchy because they stayed up too late watching TV and not knowing when to go to bed.

Day shift folk tend to think of themselves as better than the rest. They typically do have the most experience and technical knowledge. But being the superior group that they are, they often tend to leave the more distasteful aspects of the job to second shift. They see second shift as a service to them.

Sometimes it was hard to even get a cursory report from the day shift elite as to what was even going on. At times I would be shunned, like they didn't want to give me any advantages, as we were used to kicking their ass all over the place in output.

Personally, I always wanted everyone to be the best they can be. Anything else, such as intentionally hiding information, is evil.

Your experiences shape your opinions. My worldview makes me see things differently, or some would say weirdly, which is probably evident.

Den Warren

I have considered the difference in shifts, even while watching space operas.

There is no day or night at the final frontier. Yet, man cannot stay awake 24/7. So clearly there must be an off shift running those massive interplanetary space ships going all over the galaxy and beyond.

Is there a second shift working these space hulks? Obviously yes; but they don't bother telling you about it, since they are all about day shift. Fortunately for you, I am here to enlighten you on all that.

One of the main reasons you never hear about the second shift on a starship is because not much happens. Why? Not because the belligerent alien races are sleeping too, but because those baddies know not to screw around with those radical second shift crews.

While the nervous Captain on day shift will try to pal up with their creeps in the neighborhood, the second shift ensign will put an atomic torpedo up their exhaust port at the smallest provocation.

Second shift officers are used to having to deal with everything on their own. Senior officers are all over the place early in second shift to when they want to complain about the smallest detail on the previous second shift. Conversely, when there's a problem on an off shift, it's tough to get anyone from first shift to answer their freaking communicator after they go home. Day shift thinks that second shift is just a party shift, just because on a Friday they may hail a pizza merchant vessel for their lunch.

Rancid Tales

The floors on those starships really shine on the inside, but did you ever see any cleaning going on during the show? Doubt it. They are too good on day shift to allow a sanitation techie to get in their way. But on the off shifts they have to put up with mop handles accidently hitting self-destruct sequence buttons, or 409 getting into the drive turbines.

Second shift always gets the greenest cadets. Then when they are trained up to do a decent job, they want to go to day shift, or at least third shift. That is why you never see people on the sci-fi shows cussing after they push a wrong button, even though push them at crazy fast speeds while hardly looking at them. It's not like at the checkout counter when the clerk has to ask for help from the manager to clear out their faux pas.

You never see day shift spacemen arguing that they were never trained properly on firing weapons or operating anything after they monkeyed it all up.

All this about second shift, but what about third shift? Third shift is populated by a zombie race that does not understand the concept of day or night. They are immune to alien assimilation, because the aliens cannot distinguish the third shifters from themselves.

Third shift's whole purpose is to do everything possible to make life better for day shift. You know, reload all the torpedo bays, change the batteries on the shuttles, etc., etc.. Third shift has to fine tune the engines and finish patching up damage from enemy lasers, etc. All this so day shift can spend the next day tearing stuff up and getting the last bit of power possible from the engines, bringing the whole ship on the brink of destruction.

"I'm giving you all she's got! She's gonna blow, Captain!"

"Second shift will have to clean it up."

Maybe you don't see anything about those on the off shifts, because there is no such thing. They are just a figment of an alternate parallel universe, apart from the normal day shift space-time continuum.

Laundered Funds

One of the companies I worked at had its own in-house laundry. I would get a garment out of there each day to wear over my street clothes.

On one occasion, which was payday, I mistakenly left my paycheck envelope in the pocket of my smock when I turned it back into the laundry.

The next day I was called into the office. The production manager was angry because his other supervisors were all complaining that I made a lot more money than they did.

Sadly, people tend to get into trouble to the extent of what the fallout of their action is, and not to the extent of what they actually did. So therefore, it was like I was revealing to the whole Company what my rate of pay was, not that I merely left my unopened pay envelope in the laundry.

My response to him was that my privacy was violated since the envelope was unopened. All they had to do was to return it to me unopened but they did not. Now I was being badgered because of it. So instead he ended up apologizing to me over the whole thing and told me not to worry about it.

Clown Memo

When we made frozen pizzas, we made our own dough. If the dough was bad for some reason, we would put it in 55 gallon barrels, leaving some empty space because the dough would rise.

Then for some reason, we would stretch wrap the top of the barrels. It seemed like a waste of time and wrap since the scrap had its own clean room and nothing but waste food was in there. I suppose some hands-off manager thought the wrap would keep it from rising over the top and falling all over. Anyone who has ever worked with dough knows that all you have to do is punch it once in awhile, and it will nicely collapse about halfway down. You can't keep stretch wrap in it while punching.

At least one other company I worked with sold their junk dough to a hog farmer. That was back when they raised the hogs to be as fat as possible. Before pork was the "other white meat."

The management at this place was tyrannical. They would threaten to fire someone for a wide array of things, and often carried it out. Perhaps being fired from there was a blessing without any disguise.

Once day a guy back in the scrap room decided casually to amuse himself by taking his finger and drawing a clown face on the stretch wrap on a barrel. The whimsical artwork did in no way damage anything, or demean the reputation of the Company.

Well. . .this would never be tolerated! In fact, the next day a memo came out with the threat that when the person was discovered who drew the clown face, they would be fired. It certainly had to be one of the stupidest memos ever written in American industry.

    I saved the memo, along with several others in the same category. The funny thing about the stupidorandums is that they almost always threatened to fire someone.

    I think someone told the author of the memos that I was collecting the goofy things and they dried up at the source.

    I think I know who the stretch wrap artist was, but I would never dream of turning them in for something like that. If the perp was who I thought, he was a hard working valuable employee who only succumbed to a moment of boredom.

Water Hose Battles

One of the plants I worked at used a great deal of water. High pressure hot water was used by the sanitors in the plant to clean everything. The hot water was generated by turning on the cold water, then opening a valve to mix steam with it. If you did not turn the steam off first, then turn off the water, you would sometimes get a very loud blast of steam coming out. Or, if a kink got into a hose the water would block, but the steam would come out with a lot of force. It was not all that uncommon for it to happen. It wasn't that dangerous, because you could feel the steam on its way. The noise could be very startling at times for others.

So naturally, some people would create the effect on purpose. One guy called it "Crack-A-Hose". A particular dough mixer operator used to complain about this guy a lot. He would see her sleeping at the dough mixer. There was a hose station right behind her. He would open the water, and turn on the steam. Then he would turn off the water as fast as possible, leaving the steam on. It would make an incredibly loud noise. She would wake up and act like nothing happened.

Sometimes sanitors would get into vicious water fights with the hoses. Then, on occasion, it resulted in hand-to-hand combat.

One of the best battles I saw was a guy somehow got pushed onto a large turntable, about ten feet across. It spun like a merry-go-round. The victim was getting hosed off all the while he was rolling around on the table trying to get his balance.

Den Warren

I did not want to get into trouble water fighting. I knew when I was cleaning around an ambush point to listen for other hoses around the corner. If I heard one go on, I had a few seconds to act. I would position myself to soak them before they even got around the corner to see me. Armando, (from Canadian Adventure) got the worst of it. (retaliation from the wrestling match) When I was getting them, I kept getting them until they were almost drowning. He didn't know how I did it. I kept my tactics secret, and everyone pretty much left me out of it.

Note: Horseplay is very dangerous. Don't do it or encourage it.

Turning Stupid: I was in the dark break room. The break room had a partition. Someone came in the other side. Another person came in. I couldn't see either one of them. The next thing I heard was one of them threatening to kill the other because he was bad mouthing the quality of the drugs he has sold him. It was very scary. If I would have went out the door they would have seen me. I thought It was a matter of time before one of them came over to see. At least I could behave as if I heard nothing. But they never came over or knew I was in there.

Federal Agents

Any company that produces food products with meat in them, and crosses State lines must be subject to Federal Inspection. USDA inspectors wield a lot of power. They wear badges and are law enforcement officers.

Over the years, I have found that these people are fairly even-handed and reasonable with their requests.

It was my responsibility to stay on their good side as much as possible. Some of the companies with their authoritarian culture thought it best to be adversarial towards these authorities. Some of my bosses would bad mouth these people and do things just to make them mad. One USDA inspector, who was worthy of respect, told me he was torn between hammering our company for the stupid stuff our upper management was doing, but said he had to show mercy because I was so accommodating. I was grateful that he took out his wrath on someone else.

The USDA inspector assigned to me was partnered with a woman USDA inspector who was actually a former Marine Corps drill instructor. If she asked you a question, you better not quibble or obfuscate, or the hammer would be down.

These two eventually inflicted a major punishment down on the Company. It is called PEA (Progressive Enforcement Action) When PEA is in effect, you cannot run any product whatsoever with meat in it unless they are present. Plus there are often more of them assigned to the Company. The Company had to pay for the inspector's salaries. So if they all decide to leave for lunch or something, they can shut down the plant.

If someone chose to ignore that, they could come back and tell you to scrap everything you ran. It was not a happy situation. During this PEA, they told me it was okay for me to run without them around. I was pleased with that.

In other places I have run into tyrannical USDA inspectors. If you give someone that kind of power over others, sooner or later they will abuse it. This woman was bucking for some kind of promotion or something. She would not ever leave without finding at least one thing wrong. It was always some annoying regulation that cost money and did nothing to improve food quality. As far as food quality is concerned, the USDA should be the least of a food company's worries.

One time this woman inspector thought she got us on a regulation in her book. The regulation said that we "should" do something. This action made us scrap a bunch of product that was perfectly edible. It had something to do with an older label or something.

I found out about it after the damage was done. I didn't want her to get us again, so I reminded her that a "should" regulation was somewhat optional, unlike a "shall" regulation. She read it again and saw that I was right.

She clearly did not like being wrong. It was not long after that she found something to bitch about. I had someone put some broth in a tank on an off shift. Since we did that before her working hours, she tagged it, and it had to be scrapped. Plus she shut down the whole plant. 98% of the plant had nothing to do with it.

I got a phone call in the morning at home about it. I think we just scrapped the broth so she would remove the tag. All that for no reason. Everything was clean.

One of the companies also had the Commercial Division of the USDA there. All they did was ensure that our drained weights of our canned goods were correct. They were an optional service that we chose to have so we could put the USDA shield on the label.

I doubt if there was any marketing advantage to having that tiny 10mm shield on the label.

Our inspector on second shift, who we called "Ned the Fed", was a goof who lived three states away and commuted home every weekend. Sometimes he would overstep his authority and try to enforce things he had no jurisdiction over. We used to tell him that we needed to get rid of the shield from our products. He would always tell us how great the shield was for us. Overall, we got along fine with the guy.

Den Warren

Lurch

I have a weakness regarding bullies and those who choose to operate through intimidation. The problem is that I can't stand them and I want to confront them.

There was a huge guy we worked with who we used to call "Lurch". He was a part time bouncer when he wasn't working with us. Lurch was stoic, unfriendly and a goon who loved to intimidate people, as well as complain to get his way. Also, he would love to stick his nose into everything and tell us what we were doing wrong.

One time, my partner on the egg roll filling line tipped over a huge top-heavy bin of diced celery. I went to his aid to help pick it up while he was still keeping the line full. Then I noticed that we had no shovel to scoop it up with.

Meanwhile, Lurch had a separate shovel for each of his ingredients. He was the only person who worked that way. So I went over and asked him if I could borrow one of his shovels. If anything he could have been helping us out.

He said, "No."

I shook my head and said he didn't need them all right now. Then I took one. The big troll became furious and grabbed me around the neck. I just looked at him and thought about bashing him with the shovel. Not the smartest tactical move on his part.

Just then a manager walked by and saw what was going on.

We bypassed the office and went straight up to the personnel office. There were about a half-dozen managers in there and the union representatives.

The human resources manager said, "So I hear we have a couple of banty roosters out there."

I told him, "I don't appreciate your characterization when I was just getting strangled."

"You guys were fighting."

I asked him, "What are you talking about? There was no fight. If there was, he would be laying out on the floor right now."

Lurch did not like that comment.

The argument went in circles. The HR manager said we were fighting but he couldn't prove it. So then he said we would both be written up.

I told him, "So what you are saying is, if I stand up right now and walk over and strangle you, even if you don't resist, we will both be disciplined, right?"

That comment got some snickers out of some of the other managers. The cowardly HR manager just sat there dumbfounded staring at me. I didn't blink.

The cowards did write both of us up for fighting. The Union jerk was happy, figuring that he did his job since no one got fired. I told the managers that did the actual writing that they were screwing up. I suspect management later on decided I was on the wrong side.

Lurch apologized and thanked me for not being mad at him and not trying to get him fired. I told him I was sorry about the whole thing too.

Some days later I challenged him to an arm wrestling match. All of the guys gathered around. They said I had no chance and that I shouldn't do it since I would lose, which they didn't want. I figured with everyone thinking that, I had nothing to lose.

So we squared off on top of a barrel. It was on. We couldn't move each other. My immediate defeat did not happen. If I could defeat the big goon I would be a legend. . .

I smelled blood. I started to push him down, but he had an angle with that long forearm I couldn't get by. He was like pushing against a wall and allowed him to expend less energy than me. The match went on in this position for a long time. Maybe three minutes, which is a marathon in arm wrestling.

Finally, Lurch slowly sank me down and took the match. But I had given a good account of myself. Lurch never looked at me the same way again. We both got along a lot better after the write ups and the match.

Of course, today arm wrestling would be seen as horseplay or fighting. Don't do it at work.

Lurch knew we were only going to tolerate so much of his nonsense. We all started picking on him from time to time. One guy shut the lights off on him when he was in the cooler and locked the door.

They let him out, but instead of feeling threatened, he felt more like a part of the team. He just blew it off without even saying anything.

Real Clean

I have been both a sanitor and the Plant Sanitation Manager. Most people have little idea what is involved with such a job. As a Plant Sanitation Manager, I did not just manage a bunch of janitors. The requirements of a clean food plant are very rigid. Also, the job has to be done before the next production shift can get started.

Here are some examples of what should be done; the drain grates on the floor should be pulled up and sanitized every day; the complete processing machinery should be free from all food particles, including the frame and underside; pumps and pipes that pull food through them must be taken apart and cleaned inside and out, or cleaned in place; everything needs sanitized before it can be used by production.

After cleaning, the area may be swabbed for bacteria. The swab analyzer reads the light given off by the bacteria to determine if it is present. If so, the machine needs re-cleaned. This adds a whole new dimension to trying to get things clean.

Not everyone wants to do this job. It is always on an off shift. The pay is generally not high. As in all jobs, someone too good to be there was on the team. You really do whatever you can to keep that person happy.

Every day the sanitation manager is responsible for everything that is cleaned by all the sanitors. If something is not cleaned properly, it can lead to high bacteria counts, and in turn, lost product, if not food borne illness.

Den Warren

Noodle Seizure

One of my many jobs was to make noodle dough. Once per week we made rice noodles. They were tasty little things that went into the fryer after my machine cranked them out.

All I had to do to make them is to push a barrel of rice noodle flour under the vacuum which sucked it up into the mixer. Then I had to watch the amp gage. The amp gage would tell you if you had the correct amount of water in the mixer. If the gage was running too low, that meant the mixer was turning too easily because it was too wet. Conversely, if the gage was running too high, it meant the water was too low.

Never, I mean NEVER, let the mixer run out of water! If the mixer ran out of water, the screw in the machine would tie up.

There were paddles that kneaded the dough, then the clumps of dough would drop down into a long screw, which would thoroughly mix the dough and force the dough through a die. The die had tiny holes and allowed the noodles to squirt through.

A rotating blade would cut the noodles off. I had to watch the speed of the blade, which controlled the length of the noodles.

One day I was merrily watching the gage and vacuuming the barrels of rice flour. The gage went high, so I opened the water valve some more. I did some other tasks and noticed the amps was higher yet. Wow. I better open up the water some more.

I watched the gage and it still kept going up. What the. . .

With a real sense of urgency, I went up and added water directly into the mixer with a bucket. But it was too late! The dreaded screw soon groaned to a halt. I tried to manually turn the screw with a steel bar at an access point. It was frozen into place as if it were concrete.

Then I let my team leader know about the unfortunate event. He could not get it going either. He knew the screw would need pressed out with a jack. "AAAAAAAG!"

Unfortunately, the mixer was bound up exceptionally bad. No jack there at the company would get it broken free. All of the downtime and expense of everyone involved was my fault. Of course, some of the jokers thought it was a real hoot.

After spending hours on the situation, maintenance went out and rented a 60 ton jack. That could not get it out either! So they went back and got a 100 ton jack. This was the difference in weight between a medium sized army tank and a heavy army tank.

"Crap!" This was getting on my nerves in the worst way.

Fortunately, with the monster jack, the thing finally gave way. I had to clean up the entire line afterwards.

I was called into the office. I contended that I was watching the stupid thing when it jammed up and tried to add water. The shift manager contended that if I was it would have never tied up. So I was written up for poor job performance. That was a crushing blow to me. I had never had that kind of negative feedback for any of my work.

Den Warren

The next week it was time to do rice noodles again. Same product, same equipment. It only ran on second shift for some reason. I was determined that the problem would never happen again.

It wasn't too long after I started the machine that the gage was going up. I opened the valve, but it still went up...up...up. Bullcrap! I stood right there and opened it all the way.

The needle stayed up, so I shut everything down and got the crew leader. The water was put into the mixer by a pump so it could be regulated. I told the crew leader that the water pump was not working. He didn't believe me. We turned it on and it worked fine. Huh?

So I recovered from the mess and started again. Then it started going wrong again. I got the crew leader back for a second time and he confirmed that the pump was not working. Evidently it was working intermittently. At times it would not feed any water.

I went straight to the office and demanded that the write-up on my work record be rescinded. The shift manager agreed and did so immediately.

I did learn a lesson that night that served me well on many subsequent occasions after I had become the one evaluating other people's work. I used an extra measure of caution with the facts before I wrote anyone up.

As a supervisor, I was the least afraid to write up an employee who was caught not following the rules. It was either their pain or mine. No thank you.

But I was steadfast in the defense of those who were assumed guilty by mere conventional wisdom, or just to make an example of someone who wouldn't fight back as a scapegoat because they "all deserved it".

If I was unsure at all, even when the heat was on me to do something, I would hesitate. Sure enough, a couple of times I was right to investigate further on an incident, and I let the other supervisors know it.

The other supervisors were all big talkers about discipline when it was my people, but they were chickens when it was their turn, even when action was warranted.

Recycled Report: Another supervisor was complaining to me in the mail room that he had to compile massive reports and he knew for sure that no one read them. So he took a couple of pages that he had written and pulled an inch thick stack of random papers out of the wastebasket and put them behind his papers. He put the whole massive thing in the boss's mail slot.

Den Warren

Let's Run Some Scrap!

While I was a quality control person on second shift, I tried to prevent scrap. Also, I did my best to keep the on-hold inventory to a minimum. So I would try to determine the disposition of a lot, then have it scrapped, reworked, or released. This was an ongoing battle.

A process engineer there wanted to find out some results at various processing conditions. So he went ahead and ran pallet after pallet of scrap. On purpose! This ridiculous endeavor was extremely costly. Why would we make every effort to run efficiently and reduce cost, then pay good money to have doofuses like him running around pretending to be a genius.

Why didn't anyone stop this guy? Because he had a budget to waste?

Finally, I knew I was right, so I was ready to put a stop to his madness. So I went up to the guy and told him that I would not allow him to run anything on second shift. Then I imagined what all I would have to do to defend myself when I got to work the next day.

To my surprise, nothing was said. No one said whether I was right or wrong. The engineer was fine with me the next day and didn't bring it up. All I could do was shrug my shoulders and shake my head. Once again.

Circus Sex

I was in the office on second shift doing some paperwork when a woman came into the office with a complaint. She worked on the packing side of the line. That area was seldom a problem compared to the other areas I had to deal with.

The woman was not really in any emotional distress over the situation as she told me about it. Her complaint was that while she was working, a male coworker next to her had grabbed her on the butt and would not let go. Then the guy asked her if she wanted to have circus sex.

This stunning proposal first made me ponder what "circus sex" was. Would they dress up like clowns? Would they swing on a trapeze? Anyway, I had to take the matter seriously, so I did.

I brought the guy in separately. He was not distressed either. He readily admitted to doing it and I sent him home. I wondered if he wanted to quit anyway and thought it was an opportunity to grab a woman. I guess that was better than him coming into the office and sucker punching me in the face or something. This must have been an interesting report for personnel to read the next day.

Den Warren

Krazy Kall-Ins

At most of the places I supervised, I would take call-ins directly. People had quite a number ridiculous excuses why they did not come to work.

One woman had to donate bone marrow. One had to stay home because her babysitter shot herself. (Doesn't say much for her kids.) More than once someone had to stay home because their dog had puppies. (I admit I'm just ignorant about raising dogs, but really?) Any time anyone had kinfolk admitted to the hospital, whether the person was their aunt or whoever, they would need to miss work. Then there was this one about afterbirth, which I suppressed from my memory.

When I was a worker, I blew off work once to watch *Monday Night Football*. I did not lie. I told personnel it was for personal reasons. They asked what the personal reason was. I told them it was personal. But I did not enjoy it and I never did it again.

I had to be very sick to call in. One time I was so sick I was ready to pass out as I stood by the phone at home. The guards were goofing around not answering the phone. It took me over an hour to get them to answer. I was furious with them. They when they did, I was ten minutes late calling in and would be subject to discipline. I told the guard that he better write down that I called on time or I would bring him into the matter.

Racial Matters

It was Martin Luther King day on second shift. MLK Day was a recently established event at that time. I think MLK was a great man, worthy of all respect.

Almost half of my crew did not show up for work. Every single black person did not show up. We limped along that day and did not get much done. That loss of production put us into having to work Saturday.

I didn't say anything about it until the day before MLK day the following year. I asked a couple of the main opinion makers of the group if MLK was all about missing work. Also, I asked if the rest of us were supposed to have more respect for those who don't show up for work, because all it did was make us feel separated.

Sometimes people exploit the motivation of others to the extent that they could have their own way. Yes, I would rather avoid the subject too. To me, race shouldn't be a factor in anything. But someone always has to try. Why wouldn't they? They try everything else.

For example, a black worker kept missing work time and time again for the same tooth. I asked him, "Why don't you get an appointment and get that thing taken care of?"

He told me, "You sound like you are a little bit prejudiced."

"What does that have to do with anything? And another thing; telling me that I am prejudiced is very offensive. If you do it again, I will send you home."

Den Warren

I guess the guy was used to saying that kind of stuff and probably scared off most of the people he used it on. To me, that is evil. He didn't pursue further accusations of bigotry, so I did not have to make good on my threat, which maybe would have stirred the pot in the minds of some.

Another time I was on a committee with workers from another of our plants from a distant State. Priscilla was some kind of facilitator for the committee. One of the other people on the committee was a black woman. To her, every time I disagreed with her, which was often, was taken as racially motivated. I knew as a supervisor, that her ideas would never be accepted, and told her as much. She kept with the racial comments which really did make me more angry, which in turn she attributed to racial hostility.

Race had nothing to do with the fact that she didn't know what the hell she was talking about. Since her ideas would not stand up to logic, she would always take refuge on the race thing again.

Based upon what I heard her say in the past, I know with all certainty my boss Priscilla had a prejudicial negative idea of black people, which made her sound ignorant. Yet during our meeting, she acted like she was the high-minded person who was going to help steer me in the right direction.

When the meeting ended the black woman offered to shake hands and made the crude comment that the black wouldn't rub off. Very insulting, for sure. I was so sick of her, I said I wanted no more to do with the committee.

Evidently Priscilla was out badmouthing me again, since people who had nothing to do with the committee seemed to know all about it. Our maintenance manager at the Company, an openly avowed drug user, was going around telling black people that I was afraid of them. What a dope.

Racism at work is not only illegal and ugly, it is stupid. Business is supposed to run as efficiently as possible. The evil practice of excluding a valuable human resource because of race is self-defeating. Likewise, forcing any action at work solely based on race has the same effect.

Personally, I have always loved diversity in race and nationality. I have learned foreign languages. Diversity is what makes life interesting, and gives people freedom.

Den Warren

Executive Secretaries

There used to be a lot more secretaries around. They have been either replaced by computers, or their boss was replaced by a computer and the more capable secretaries had become the boss.

The old situation where the grossly underpaid woman secretary was paired with the man boss was one which worked unfairly against women. If the secretary was a go-getter, The man got all of her ideas and work, and then he got all of the credit and pay.

I don't see the situation being that way as much anymore, although I know it is not extinct.

It was a stark contrast. They sat at a nice desk. They had nice clothes. They had tidy hair. They had close proximity to the boss. All the things the production supervisors did not. It only stands to reason, at least to them, that they were more important.

We production supervisors came into the office and looked like a wreck. We wore uniforms with food slop all over them, and a hair net, slopped up boots, and safety glasses. We came into the office with all kinds of horrible problems that the secretaries would figure was our own bad karma, and they would never have had such a problem if they were in charge. Of course, they learned some of this posturing from their bosses.

Human resource administrative personnel were often crusading against us supervisors as malevolent beings who loved to run off their precious valuable hirelings. Every time we would become short-handed our pain was compounded by HR complaining about us, and our boss listening to them.

Admittedly, there were cases where HR was spot on with their assessment of some supervisors, who could have used some more training or a kick in the pants. But these cases were not the norm. It is a huge difficulty to be short-handed.

It would be helpful if people were required to use some sort of objective criteria to back up their claims. All their information was hearsay as they had no practical experience with anything. They couldn't tell you the difference between a cooker and blancher.

Often times, the executive secretaries were the worst. If they were a manipulative type of person, as so many at all levels are in the workplace, they would use their proximity and time with the boss to fulfill their personal agenda. Feeling themselves to be on the same level as a vice-president, sometimes they would advise the boss on what we supervisors were doing wrong, or just making sure the boss knew everything bad that we lowly supervisors were up to.

These self-important administrative people must have been eating their hearts out when they saw how much more we supervisors were paid. If they didn't like their situation, there were plenty of more boots and hairnets to go around.

Den Warren

Betrayal

One of my workers got into trouble for absenteeism. It went to the level of termination of employment. During his time with the Company he desperately wanted raises, which I felt were justified, so I tried to get them for him. I was able to get some improvement for him.

For some reason, during his exit interview, he decided to make me look as bad as possible. He said that I was knowingly allowing rat dung to be put on the product and he came up with a whole shopping list of complaints he had about me. He had a number of other out and out lies on the list, and I did not understand why he did it.

Then he came back one day and asked if I would give him a good reference for another job. I asked him about what happened with his exit interview and he withdrew his reference request.

So many times I have been lied about by others for their own benefit. When I started in supervision, I considered myself to be a people person. Eventually I came to the point where I no longer wanted to be a supervisor. I did not want to deal with anyone's problems other than my own.

Human Resource Consultants

At least a couple of times while working in the food industry over the years, the company would send all of the supervisors to an outside venue at a motel conference room. We were to get together and figure out what needed to be done to get better.

Usually, it ended up being a session to compile a list of grievances against upper management. So naturally, nothing ever changed from the sessions as upper management was "already doing all they can."

Our parent Corporation bought out another large company that was failing. The unit I worked at was put into a new division under the failing company.

Our new division had one of these meetings. Because of the changes they had forced upon us, we started running so poorly that it seemed like they wanted us to go out of business.

That meeting is where we were introduced to the concept of signing off on a document that we would agree to do certain things that we were told to do. That was an alien concept to us. We always did what we were told anyway, and it seemed to question our integrity. It was never explained to us why we had to sign papers saying we would do what we already agreed to do. We were insulted. Some chose not to be a signatory to the agreement. The Company held that against those who refused, and they were laid off with a year.

www.ingramcontent.com/pod-product-compliance
Lightning Source LLC
Chambersburg PA
CBHW051727170526
45167CB00002B/835